UCHICAGO **Consortium**
on School Research

I0220670

RESEARCH REPORT NOVEMBER 2017

Chicago's Charter High Schools

Organizational Features, Enrollment, School Transfers, and Student Performance

Julia A. Gwynne and Paul T. Moore

TABLE OF CONTENTS

ACKNOWLEDGEMENTS

The authors gratefully acknowledge the many people who contributed to this report. The study would not have been possible without generous funding from the CME Group Foundation, Crown Family Philanthropies, and an anonymous funder. Our colleague at the UChicago Consortium, Jennie Jiang, was an invaluable member of our research team and contributed to the study in many important ways. The study also benefitted from feedback from a number of different people, including a local advisory committee of education stakeholders in Chicago and a national advisory committee of experts on charter schools. The local advisory committee included Daniel Anello, Michael Beyer, Mary Bradley, Kyle Cole, Catherine Deutsch, Shayne Evans, Kevin Gallick, Sagar Gokhale, Kurt Hilgendorf, Nicole Howard, Sarah Howard, Seth Kaufman, Matt King, Lila Leff, Gerald Lui, Beatriz Ponce de León, and Maurice Swinney. The national advisory committee included Julian Betts, Linda Renzulli, and Steve Rivken. Other Consortium colleagues, including Elaine Allensworth, David Johnson, Kylie Klein, Jenny Nagaoka, Penny Sebring, and Marisa de la Torre, provided helpful feedback at all stages of this report. In addition, Todd Rosenkranz conducted a very thorough technical read of the report, and the UChicago Consortium's communications team, including Bronwyn McDaniel, Jessica Tansey, Jessica Puller, and R. Steven Quispe were instrumental in the production of this report. We are also grateful to members of our Steering Committee, including Gina Caneva, Catherine Deutsch, Raquel Farmer-Hinton, and Beatriz Ponce de León, for their thoughtful reviews and comments on an earlier draft of this report. We also gratefully acknowledge the Spencer Foundation and the Lewis-Sebring Family Foundation, whose operating grants support the work of the UChicago Consortium. The UChicago Consortium greatly appreciates support from the Consortium Investor Council that funds critical work beyond the initial research: putting the research to work, refreshing the data archive, seeding new studies, and replicating previous studies. Members include: Brinson Family Foundation, CME Group Foundation, Crown Family Philanthropies, Lloyd A. Fry Foundation, Joyce Foundation, Lewis-Sebring Family Foundation, McDougal Family Foundation, Osa Family Foundation, Polk Bros. Foundation, Spencer Foundation, Steans Family Foundation, and The Chicago Public Education Fund.

Cite as: Gwynne, J.A., & Moore, P.T. (2017). *Chicago's charter high schools: Organizational features, enrollment, school transfers, and student performance.* Chicago, IL: University of Chicago Consortium on School Research.

This report was produced by the UChicago Consortium's publications and communications staff: Bronwyn McDaniel, Director of Outreach and Communication; Jessica Tansey, Communications Manager; Jessica Puller, Communications Specialist, and R. Steven Quispe, Development and Communications Coordinator.

Graphic Design: Jeff Hall Design
Photography: Eileen Ryan and Cynthia Howe
Editing: Jessica Puller, Katelyn Silva, and Jessica Tansey

11.2017/350/jh.design@rcn.com

Executive Summary

The rapid growth of charter schools in the Chicago Public Schools (CPS) has changed the landscape of public education in the city. As of 2016, 22 percent of CPS students in grades 9–12 were enrolled in a charter high school, compared to only 4 percent a decade earlier. As schools that receive public funds, but retain independence from some types of regulation, charter schools occupy a distinct niche, one that has led to ongoing debate both nationally and locally about their role in public education.

Much of this debate has focused on whether student achievement in charter schools is higher than in traditional public schools. In response, numerous studies in districts around the country have examined charter school performance over the past 20 years. Most of these studies have focused exclusively on test score performance. Early studies typically showed that charter school students had similar test scores, or in some cases, somewhat lower scores, than their peers in traditional public schools. More recently, a number of studies have found that charter students, particularly those enrolled in urban charter schools, have significantly higher test scores than similar students in traditional public schools.[1]

Although there is abundant research on charter schools nationally, few rigorous studies have examined the performance of charter schools in Chicago, and those that have relied on relatively small samples of students.[2] Despite the scarcity of local research, supporters of Chicago's charter schools point to publicly-available test score data as evidence that some charter schools do a better job educating students than non-

charter schools. But critics question whether these results could be driven by problematic practices within charter schools, such as enrolling mostly high-performing students while simultaneously counseling out any low-performing students who enroll. Amidst the debate over charter school performance in Chicago and across the country, virtually no research has compared student performance on other important indicators, like academic behaviors, attendance, and grades—despite the fact that grades and attendance have been shown to be more predictive than test scores for outcomes such as high school and college graduation, and even lifetime earnings.[3]

This study is the first in-depth look at Chicago's charter schools by the University of Chicago Consortium on School Research (UChicago Consortium). We examined four key dimensions of charter high schools in CPS: school organization and policies; incoming skills and characteristics of charter high school enrollees; school transfers; and student performance. We began by first looking at the organizational capacity and policies of charter schools. Charter schools may differ from

---

1   See, for example, Zimmer & Buddin (2006); Bifulco & Ladd (2006); Center for Research on Education Outcomes (2009; 2013; 2015); Zimmer, Gill, Booker, Lavertu, Sass, & Witte (2009); Hoxby, Murarka, & Kang (2009); Abdulkadiroglu, Angrist, Dynarski, Kane, & Pathak (2011); Harris & Larsen (2016).

2   See, for example, Booker, Sass, Gill, & Zimmer (2008); Hoxby & Rockoff (2004).

3   Allensworth & Easton (2005; 2007); Balfanz, Herzog, & MacIver (2007); Bowers (2010); Bowen, Chingos, & McPherson (2009); Camara & Echternacht (2000); Geiser & Santelices (2007); Hoffman & Lowitzki (2005); Rothstein (2004).

traditional public schools in terms of their mission and practices, but whether they are organized differently on dimensions that matter for student learning is not known. Using the five essential supports framework, which CPS and other districts around the country use to understand school practices, we examined whether charter schools differed from non-charter schools in the five essentials categories: instructional leadership, collaborative teachers, involved families, supportive environment, and ambitious instruction. We also looked at some charter schools' policies related to student learning—such as the number of instructional days and requirements for promotion and graduation—to see how they differed from non-charter schools.

We then explored who enrolled in charter schools to examine the concern that charter schools in Chicago may be enrolling mostly high-performing students. We compared each charter high school's enrollees on a range of eighth-grade indicators—including test scores, grades, attendance, and study habits—to students who came from the same elementary schools and neighborhoods as charter students but enrolled in different high schools. We also examined the relationship between characteristics of charter schools—including their academic reputations and safety—and the incoming qualifications of the students who enrolled.

Next, we looked at charter high schools' transfer rates to assess the concern that students in these schools may be more likely to transfer out of their ninth-grade schools than students enrolled in non-charter high schools. In addition, we examined the relationship between the academic performance of schools and their students' transfer rates.

We then examined charter school students' performance on a range of outcomes in high school—including attendance, classroom engagement, study habits, grit, test scores, promotion to tenth grade, and high school graduation—and college—including enrollment in a four-year college or university, enrollment in a very selective college or university, and completion of four semesters of college.

Finally, we looked at how much variation exists among charter schools on key outcomes, including students' test scores, college enrollment rates, and enrollment in very selective colleges or universities.

Most of the research on charter schools focuses on overall differences between this sector and traditional public schools. We examined variation among charter high schools to assess how similar or different they are from one another.

This study relied primarily on data from 2010, 2011, 2012, and 2013. Analyses of charter schools' organizational capacity examined teacher and student survey responses from these years. Analyses of students' incoming skills and characteristics, school transfers, and high school outcomes were based on students who were first-time ninth-graders in each of these years. However, many of these students had not yet had sufficient time to graduate from high school and transition to post-secondary opportunities when this study was conducted; to address this, we used a second group of students in our analyses of these later student outcomes; these included students who were first-time ninth-graders in 2008, 2009, and 2010. Analyses of student survey responses, school transfers, and high school and college outcomes used statistical models that controlled for a wide range of students' eighth-grade characteristics, skills, and school experiences. Appendix A provides additional details on the statistical models used in these analyses.

Key Findings

On average, CPS charter high schools looked similar to non-charter, non-selective schools on some dimensions of organizational capacity, such as leadership, but they looked quite different on other dimensions, such as instruction and preparation of students for the future. Based on survey responses, charter school teachers described their leaders in much the same way that teachers in non-charter, non-selective high schools did. They reported comparable levels of trust in their principals, and a similar willingness by their principals to promote teacher participation in establishing policies and practices. Charter school teachers also described school leaders as setting similarly high standards for teaching and learning as teachers in non-charter, non-selective schools, and they reported comparable levels of program coherence at their schools. Despite similar perceptions about school leaders, charter school teachers described relationships with colleagues as characterized by higher levels of trust and a greater sense of collective responsibility than teachers in non-charter, non-selective schools.

Charter schools looked most different from non-charter, non-selective schools in their preparation of students for the future. Typically, charter schools had more requirements for grade-level promotion and high school graduation, although most had a comparable number of instructional days as non-charter schools. Based on survey responses, charter school teachers reported greater willingness to try innovative strategies in the classroom, and students in these schools described their classes as being more academically demanding. Charter school students were also more likely to say their schools engaged all students in planning for the future, compared to similar students in non-charter schools. This aligned with reports by charter school teachers who described their schools as more likely to expect all students to attend college and to promote college readiness more than teachers in non-charter, non-selective schools.

Most CPS charter high schools enrolled students whose eighth-grade test scores were similar to or lower than students in non-charter high schools who came from their same neighborhoods and elementary schools, but whose eighth-grade attendance was higher. Using descriptive statistics, we compared each charter schools' enrollees on a range of eighth-grade indicators—including test scores, grades, attendance, and study habits—to a "feeder pool" of students who came from the same elementary schools and neighborhoods as charter students but enrolled in different high schools.[4] We found that most charter high schools enrolled students with incoming eighth-grade test scores that were either comparable to or lower than students from their feeder pool. On other measures of incoming skills and

behavior, however, a different pattern emerged. Nearly all charter high schools enrolled students with higher eighth-grade attendance than their feeder pool, and about one-third of charter high schools enrolled students whose eighth-grade GPAs were higher than their feeder pools.

Despite these overall patterns, there was a good deal of variation among charter schools in the average incoming test scores, attendance, and grades of their students. Charter high schools with strong academic reputations and safety records were more likely to attract students with higher eighth-grade test scores, attendance, and grades, relative to their feeder pools, than charter high schools with weak academic reputations and safety records.

Students who enrolled in a charter high school in ninth grade were more likely to transfer to another CPS high school than students enrolled in a non-charter high school, even after taking into account differences in incoming skills, experiences, and characteristics. Among CPS students who entered high school in 2010-13 with typical eighth-grade skills, school experiences, and background characteristics, 24.2 percent of those who enrolled in a charter school in ninth grade changed schools at some point during the next three years, compared to only 17.2 percent of students who first enrolled in a non-charter high school. Much of the debate around charter school transfers has focused on the possibility that these schools may counsel low-achieving students to enroll elsewhere, as a means of protecting their academic reputations. We found that both low- and high-achieving charter school students were more likely to change schools than non-charter students with comparable test scores. Transfer rates were highest for charter school students when they began high school in a low-performing or newly established charter school.

---

4 Typically, analyses of who enrolls in charter schools compare the incoming skills and behaviors of charter school students to all other students in the district; but this approach does not take into account the fact that most charter high schools are located in high-poverty neighborhoods, and like other high schools in CPS, serve students from the surrounding community. It is possible that charter schools could enroll a greater proportion of higher-achieving students from their communities than other nearby schools and still serve students whose achievement level is below the district average. To investigate this possibility, we compared students who enrolled in a given charter school to a "feeder pool" of students who lived in the same neighborhood as enrollees or attended the same elementary school, but who did not attend that charter school.

On average, charter school students performed better on some (but not all) high school outcomes than students enrolled in non-charter high schools, controlling for differences in incoming skills, experiences, and background characteristics. During high school, charter school students had better attendance and better test scores, on average, than students in non-charter high schools, after taking into account differences in incoming skills and characteristics. For example, among CPS students with typical incoming skills, school experiences, and background characteristics, those who enrolled in a charter high school had an attendance rate of 93 percent in ninth grade, compared to 88.5 percent for students enrolled in a non-charter high school, a difference of nearly 5 percentage points, or about eight days of school. In terms of test score performance, the typical CPS student in a charter high school scored nearly two-tenths of a standard deviation higher on the tenth-grade PLAN test and one-quarter of a standard deviation higher on the eleventh-grade ACT than the typical student in a non-charter high school. These differences are equivalent to about six-tenths of a point higher on the PLAN and a full point higher on the ACT.

On other measures of high school academic behaviors and course performance, charter school students' performance was similar to or slightly below students in non-charter schools, after taking into account differences in incoming skills and background characteristics. For example, on survey measures of study habits and grit, charter school students scored at comparable levels as similar students in non-charter schools. Their promotion rates to tenth grade within one year of entering high school—a proxy for whether students are likely to graduate from high school within four years—were around 2 percentage points lower than similar students in non-charter high schools; however, this difference may have been due to charter schools typically having more requirements for promotion than non-charter schools.

On average, charter school students' performance on post-secondary outcomes was much higher than similar students who attended non-charter high schools. In terms of educational attainment, charter high school students had comparable rates of high school graduation, but their post-secondary outcomes were generally better than students who attended non-charter high schools, after taking into account differences in incoming skills and background characteristics. For example, among CPS students who entered high school in 2008, 2009, or 2010 with typical incoming skills, school experiences, and background characteristics, the four-year college enrollment rate was 45.1 percent for those who attended a charter high school, compared to 26.2 percent for students who attended a non-charter high school. Enrollment rates in very selective colleges and universities were also higher for charter school students—7.2 percent compared to 2.2 percent for similar students who attended non-charter high schools.

Among high school graduates, charter school students were more likely to complete at least four semesters of college than students who attended a non-charter high school, after controlling for differences in incoming skills, experiences, and background characteristics—21.4 percent compared to 13.0 percent. Among college enrollees, however, charter school and non-charter school students had similar completion rates of four semesters: around 53 percent for both groups.

There was substantial variation among charter schools on key student outcomes, including test scores, college enrollment, and college selectivity. Our findings highlight that not all charter schools are the same. There was considerable variation among these schools on key student outcomes, including test scores, college enrollment, and college selectivity. In fact, once we controlled for differences in incoming skills, experiences, and background characteristics, there was far more variation among charter schools on these outcomes than among non-charter schools. Moreover, amongst the highest-performing schools, charter school performance exceeded the performance of non-charter high schools serving similar students. For example, at a small number of charter high schools, average test scores were more than 0.50 standard deviations above the district average, whereas test scores at the highest performing non-charter high schools serving similar students were only 0.30 standard deviations above the district average. Similarly, college enrollment rates for typical CPS students exceeded 70 percent in a small number of charter high schools, whereas college enrollment rates in the highest-performing non-charter schools was around 50 percent. Although enrollment rates in very selective colleges were low overall, a small number of charter schools had enrollment rates that exceeded 10 percent, again higher than the highest-performing non-charter schools serving similar students.

At the other end of the spectrum, there were a few charter schools with very low levels of performance on these outcomes; their performance was similar to the lowest-performing non-charter schools. At a time when school choice discussions are frequent, this provides an important reminder that school type does not determine school quality.

Summary

This study found that, on average, charter high schools in Chicago look similar to non-charter schools on some dimensions of organizational capacity and on some measures of student performance, but charter high schools stood out in other areas, including student attendance, test-score performance, and college outcomes. We also found considerable variation among charter high schools on key outcomes, including test scores and college outcomes. Given the range of performance among charter schools, and also among non-charter high schools, finding ways in which charter and non-charter high schools can engage in more collaboration around best practices could be beneficial. Many non-charter schools in Chicago have spent years focused on improving student course performance in an effort to increase Freshman OnTrack rates and high school graduation rates; some of these schools may have insights to share about how to promote strong academic behaviors and mindsets, such as grit and study habits. Similarly, a number of charter high schools have developed strong records promoting test score growth and college enrollment; these schools may have insights that could lead to more access to opportunities for Chicago's young people. Sharing best practices among all of Chicago's high schools—charter and non-charter—could be one way to ensure that there are strong school options—and student outcomes—in both sectors.

Introduction

Charter schools represent one of the more recent initiatives in the school choice movement. Conceived in the 1970s, but not introduced until the 1990s, charter schools were intended to be autonomous schools, created by teachers, which could pursue innovative educational practices without interference from many of the regulations to which traditional public schools are subject. The hope was that educational innovation would lead to higher levels of student achievement, particularly for low-income and minority students.[5]

Consistent with the original concept, today's charter schools are public schools open to all students but exempt from many of the regulations that traditional public schools must follow. In Illinois, for example, charter schools are free to set their own budgets; hire and fire teachers directly; and determine grade promotion and graduation requirements. They can also establish their own student discipline code, set their own academic calendar, and determine their admissions process, as long as they comply with state law governing each of these areas. But, unlike other schools of choice, such as selective enrollment schools and many magnet schools, charter schools are prohibited from having admissions requirements based on academic performance, such as minimum test scores or grades.[6]

As schools that receive public funds, but retain independence from some types of regulation, charter schools occupy a distinct niche in the educational landscape, one that has led to ongoing debate about their role in public education. A central focus of this debate has been whether charter schools have realized their promise to produce greater student learning than traditional public schools, in exchange for less regulation. A second area of concern has focused on charter schools' practices regarding enrollment.[7] Some worry that charter schools could be attracting mostly high-performing students, since it is families with higher levels of human and social capital who are best able to navigate the application process and have the time and capacity to research school options.[8] If charters are enrolling mostly high-achieving students, traditional public schools could be left with a disproportionate share of students who lack such supports. Other concerns focus on charter schools' retention of students over time and whether these schools are more likely to counsel out some students because of a lack of fit with their model.[9] Finally, questions have also been raised about whether charter schools are really as innovative as the original vision intended.[10]

In the ensuing years since charter schools first appeared, a considerable amount of research has emerged investigating many of these questions. This body of work has played an important role in helping educators, policymakers, and the public understand key dimen-

---

5   Budde (1974); Shanker (1988, March 31; 1988, July 10).
6   Charter schools in Illinois can engage in additional intake activities, such as asking for student essays, school-parent compacts, or open houses, but they cannot require participation in these activities as a condition of enrollment. (See 105 ILCS 5/27A-4 at http://www.ilga.gov/legislation/ilcs/full-text.asp?DocName=010500050K27A-4).

7   Ravitch (2016); Schemo (2004, August 17).
8   Henig (1995); Teske & Schneider (2001); Lee, Croninger & Smith (1996).
9   Brown (2013, January 5); Strauss (2012, February 2).
10 Lubienski (2003).

sions of charter schools, including who enrolls in these schools and how these students perform. Nevertheless, this research is also characterized by some limitations, including a singular reliance on test scores to measure student performance, and limited attention to differences within the charter community. This report provides an in-depth look at charter high schools and students in CPS, and examines four dimensions of charter schools—organizational features, student enrollment, school transfers, and a broad array of student outcomes—while attending to variation within the charter community.

Current Research on Charter Schools

Over the past 20 years, numerous studies have examined whether charter school students have higher levels of academic achievement than their peers in traditional public schools. Early studies found that charter school students performed at about the same level, or in some cases, below their peers in traditional public schools.[11] Recently, however, there is growing evidence that students who attend charter schools, particularly in urban areas, perform significantly better than similar students in traditional public schools.[12] Especially noteworthy is a recent national study of 41 urban districts in 22 states, which found that, on average, students enrolled in charter schools had significantly higher one-year test score gains in reading and math than their peers in traditional public schools.[13]

This body of research has provided a helpful lens for understanding charter school performance, particularly as the sector has matured over time. But its singular focus on test scores leaves many questions unanswered about other aspects of student achievement in charter schools. While test scores are an important measure of high school and college readiness, they are not the only measure of how prepared students are for the future. Other important indicators include students' grades, attendance, and other academic behaviors, such as study habits and grit. In fact, grades and attendance have been shown to be more predictive than test scores of outcomes such as high school and college graduation, and also future earnings.[14] Yet virtually no research has compared how charter school students perform relative to their peers in traditional public schools on a broader array of college-readiness indicators.

Examining how charter school students perform in terms of their educational attainment is also essential, but only a few studies have studied these outcomes. Findings on high school graduation have shown mixed results for charter schools,[15] while findings for college enrollment and persistence for at least two years in college have generally shown positive charter school effects.[16] The relative dearth of research in this area is likely due to the challenge of obtaining data from multiple institutions and also the lengthy period of time needed to build a data archive that can answer these questions. Nevertheless, these milestones are critical measures of how well high schools are serving their students, and understanding how charter school students perform in these areas are an important component of assessing their success.

Another body of research on charter schools has focused on charter school enrollment and school transfers. Despite concerns that charter schools may be enrolling mostly high-performing students, there is little research evidence confirming these concerns. For example, studies of a number of districts and states

11 See, for example, Zimmer & Buddin (2006); Bifulco & Ladd (2006); Center for Research on Education Outcomes (2009); Zimmer et al. (2009).

12 See for example, Hoxby et al. (2009); Abdulkadiroglu et al. (2011); Center for Research on Education Outcomes (2013; 2015); Harris & Larsen (2016).

13 Center for Research on Education Outcomes (2015).

14 Allensworth & Easton (2005; 2007); Balfanz et al. (2007); Bowers (2010); Bowen et al. (2009); Camara & Echternacht (2000); Geiser & Santelices (2007); Hoffman & Lowitzki (2005); Rothstein (2004).

15 Using a lottery study approach to assess charter effects, Angrist, Cohodes, Dynarski, Pathak, & Walters (2013) found that lottery winners in Boston graduated from high school at the same rates as lottery losers. Fryer & Dobbie (2015), who also conducted a study of charter lottery winners and losers, found that the four-year graduation rates of lottery winners were significantly higher than lottery losers; however, the six-year high school graduation rates showed no difference between lottery winners and losers, indicating that lottery losers were able to close the attainment gap over time. In a study of charter schools in Florida and Chicago, Booker, Sass, Gill, & Zimmer (2011) found that charter school students had high school graduation rates that were between 7 and 15 percentage points higher than students enrolled in traditional public schools.

16 Booker, Gill, Sass, & Zimmer (2014); Angrist et al. (2013); Fryer & Dobbie (2015).

have shown that charter schools enroll students with lower incoming test scores than students attending other schools in the district.[17] But again, this research has not considered other dimensions of students' incoming qualifications beyond test scores. In districts like CPS, in which there are a number of school choice options specifically targeting students with high test scores, charter schools may enroll a distinctive niche of students who do not have high test scores, but who are strong in other areas such as attendance, study habits, or grades.

Research on school transfers is less prevalent than research on charter school enrollments or performance; the few districtwide studies that have investigated this issue have found no evidence that charter school students are more likely to transfer to other schools than non-charter school students.[18] However, this research has generally not attended to variation within the charter community, nor whether students are more likely to transfer out of some charter schools than others.

There has also been relatively little research on the organizational features of charter schools. To date, most studies of charter schools' organization have focused on the practices of highly-effective charter schools.[19] Less well-understood is how charter schools are organized on dimensions that matter for student learning, such as leadership structure and collaboration, school climate, and instruction, and whether they look different on these dimensions than traditional public schools.

Another limitation of existing research on charter schools is a lack of attention to differences among charter schools. Most studies of charter school performance focus on overall differences in outcomes between charter school students and students in traditional public schools. In reality, however, it is unlikely that there is a single type of charter student or a single type of charter school. Understanding how similar or different charter schools are from one another can provide a much more informed picture of the sector overall.

This Study

This report addresses four key dimensions of charter schools—their organizational features, enrollment patterns, retention of students over time, and student performance. It brings together extensive data that includes student administrative data, survey data, interview data, and charter application data (**see box on p.11 titled, "Sources of Information about CPS Charter Schools"**). These data provide a comprehensive picture of charter schools in CPS and extend the current knowledge base about charter schools in a number of ways. The report is structured in the following way:

Chapter 1 provides a brief overview of the history of charter schools in Chicago, including their growth, the authorization process, and some of the tensions that have surrounded these schools.

Chapter 2 turns to the question of how charter schools are organized. Specifically, we asked:

• How similar or different were charter school policies regarding the number of instructional days, grade-level promotion, and graduation requirements? Using the five essential supports framework, how did charter high schools compare to non-charter high schools in terms of their effective leadership, collaborative teachers, involved families, supportive environment, and ambitious instruction?

In Chapter 3, we explore who enrolled in charter high schools and whether their incoming qualifications and characteristics differed from students from the same neighborhoods and elementary schools who enrolled in other kinds of high schools. We asked:

• How did charter high school students compare to students who enrolled in other high schools, in terms of their incoming academic skills and behaviors, course performance, and background characteristics? How were the characteristics of charter schools related to who enrolled in these schools?

17 Hoxby (2003); Zimmer et al. (2009); Garcia, McIlroy, & Barber (2008); Tuttle, Gill, Gleason, Knechtel, Nichols-Barrer, & Resch (2013).
18 Zimmer & Guarino (2013); Winters (2015).

19 These included an extended school day and year, data-driven monitoring of student performance, and a culture of high expectations (Almond, 2012; Dobbie & Fryer, 2013).

Chapter 4 examines charters schools' transfer rates of students over time. It also looks at the relationship between the academic performance of charter schools and how likely students are to transfer out of them. We asked:

- Were charter school students more or less likely to transfer out of their school than similar students enrolled in other high schools? Did charter school students transfer rates differ depending on the academic performance of the school in which they enrolled?

Chapter 5 compares charter school students' performance to similar students who enrolled in non-charter schools on a range of high school indicators, including ninth- and eleventh-grade attendance, study habits, persistence, classroom engagement, on-time promotion to tenth grade, and test scores. We also analyze sector differences in students' educational attainment, including high school graduation, college enrollment, college selectivity, and college persistence. We asked:

- How did charter high school students compare in terms of their high school performance and educational attainment to similar students in other schools? How much variation was there among charter schools in terms of their students' high school performance and educational attainment?

Chapter 6 offers an interpretive summary of the key findings of the report and highlights implications for policy and practice for both charter and non-charter schools.

This study relied on two analytic samples. The primary sample included four cohorts of first-time ninth-graders from 2010-11 through 2013-14 who were enrolled in a CPS high school in ninth grade and who were also enrolled in CPS for eighth grade the year prior, a total of 103,506 students in 147 high schools, of which 46 were charter schools.[20] This sample was used for analyses of organizational features of charter and non-charter high schools (Chapter 2), incoming

skills and characteristics (Chapter 3), school transfers (Chapter 4), and high school outcomes (Chapter 5). Because most of these students had not yet had sufficient time to transition to and through college when this study was conducted, we used a second sample for analyses of educational attainment (Chapter 5). This sample included three cohorts of students who were first-time ninth-graders from 2008-09 through 2010-11, a total of 81,257 students enrolled in 133 high schools, of which 36 are charter schools. There was a good deal of overlap between the two samples: all but one of the 36 charter high schools from the earlier sample were included in the primary sample; and one of the cohorts, students who were first-time ninth-graders in 2010, was also included in both samples.

A Note About Our Research Methods

When studying the performance of charter schools, it is important to take into account differences between students who enroll in these schools and other students in the district. Students and their families who choose to attend a school other than their neighborhood school may be more motivated to ensure educational success than students and families who did not make a similar choice, and this kind of motivation can have an impact on student performance. Many studies of charter schools address this selection bias through the use of lottery studies. These studies are considered the "gold-standard" for addressing this kind of bias because they compare two groups of students who are similarly motivated to attend a charter school: those who win the lottery and those who lose the lottery. In CPS, however, only around one-half of all charter schools run lotteries (schools that are not oversubscribed have no need to run a lottery). Research has shown that oversubscribed charter schools are generally higher-performing than undersubscribed charter schools.[21] Given this, limiting our study to only those charter schools that run lotteries would likely mean that findings would not be representative of all charter high schools in the district.

---

20 We excluded special education and alternative schools, including all charter alternative schools (e.g., Youth Connections Schools). We also excluded Chicago Virtual Charter School, which offered online classes. Given that the educational experiences of students in this school were likely to be completely different from students attending regular charter high schools, we elected not to include it in our analyses.

21 Angrist, Pathak, & Walters (2013).

Our approach to analyzing charter school performance allowed us to compare charter school students to similar students in non-charter schools. We used an extensive set of information about students prior to their entry into high school, including their background characteristics, academic performance, whether they attended a neighborhood school, and the characteristics of their eighth-grade school, including quality and climate. Because the information on students is so comprehensive, it likely addresses any selection bias that may have impacted charter school students' outcomes.[22] A precedent for this approach exists in a small, but growing, number of studies that show methods using regression controls or statistical matching produce results that are quite similar to lottery-based methods using the same data.[23] **Appendix A** provides additional details about our research methods.

Sources of Information about CPS Charter Schools

Administrative Data: In partnership with CPS, the UChicago Consortium has developed an extensive data archive that includes information about students' background characteristics (e.g., gender, race/ethnicity, grade, age, school), test scores, course performance,[A] attendance, and reasons for leaving CPS (e.g., graduation, dropping out, transferring). Students' residential addresses are linked to census data and Chicago Police Department data on crimes, allowing for nuanced information about the socioeconomic conditions in students' neighborhoods. CPS student IDs have also been linked to National Student Clearinghouse data, which provides information about post-secondary enrollment.

Survey Data: During the spring of each year, CPS administers the *My Voice, My School* survey to all teachers in the district and to students in grades 6–12. For this study, we used teacher and student responses on surveys administered in the spring of 2011, 2012, 2013, and 2014, the same school years in which our primary analytic sample were in their first year in high school. Survey responses were used to describe the organizational capacity of charter and non-charter high schools and also the experiences of students in these schools. Response rates on the student surveys in those years exceeded 70 percent in each year. Response rates on the teacher survey were 48.6 percent in 2011, 65.4 percent in 2012, 81.1 percent in 2013, and 80.9 percent in 2014.

Interviews: We interviewed 27 charter leadership members across eight Charter Management Organizations (CMOs) and individual schools. Data collected from interviews were not intended to be representative, but rather to highlight common challenges, successes, and strategies shared by charter leaders.

Charter School Data: Information about charter schools' policies and practices came from annual reports submitted by charter schools to CPS, as stipulated by charter school law. These data included information about the length of the school year and school day, as well as requirements for promotion to tenth grade and for high school graduation.

A   Many CPS charter schools use different student information systems from the IMPACT system used by non-charter schools. Because each system varies in the way that it stores information about courses, credits, teachers, periods, grades, and other data, creating linkages across systems is difficult, and our data archive currently does not include records of charter school students' course performance.

---

22 We also performed a validation study, described in Appendix A, using the same set of data in which charter school students were matched with students attending traditional public schools on a variety of pre-treatment characteristics (similar to the CREDO studies (2013, 2015) and it yielded very similar results.

23 Angrist et al. (2013); Abdulkadiroğlu et al. (2011); Dobbie & Fryer (2013); Deming (2014).

FIGURE 1

A Brief Timeline of Key Points in CPS Charter School History

ILLINOIS

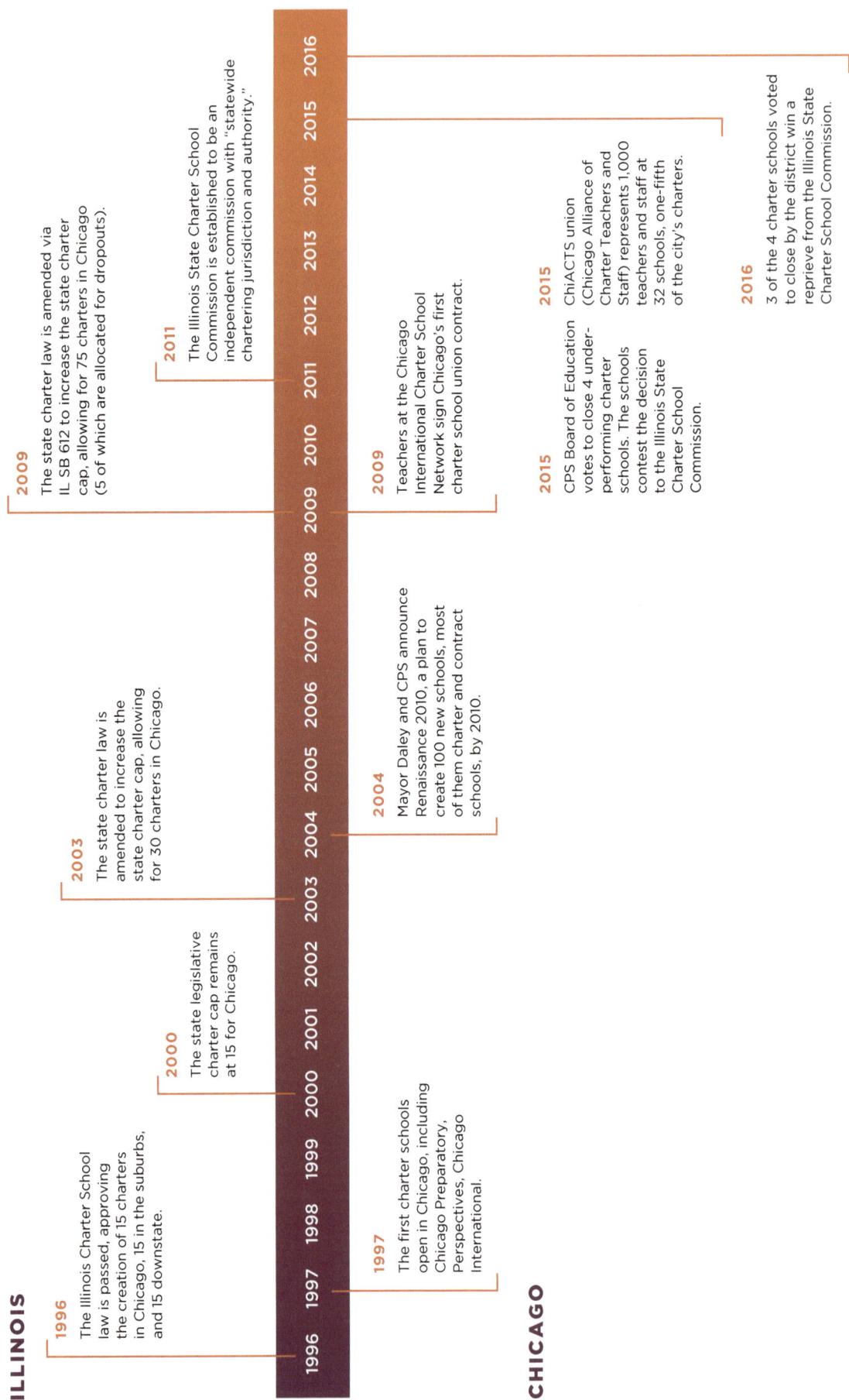

1996
The Illinois Charter School law is passed, approving the creation of 15 charters in Chicago, 15 in the suburbs, and 15 downstate.

2000
The state legislative charter cap remains at 15 for Chicago.

2003
The state charter law is amended to increase the state charter cap, allowing for 30 charters in Chicago.

2009
The state charter law is amended via IL SB 612 to increase the state charter cap, allowing for 75 charters in Chicago (5 of which are allocated for dropouts).

2011
The Illinois State Charter School Commission is established to be an independent commission with "statewide chartering jurisdiction and authority."

1996 1997 1998 1999 2000 2001 2002 2003 2004 2005 2006 2007 2008 2009 2010 2011 2012 2013 2014 2015 2016

CHICAGO

1997
The first charter schools open in Chicago, including Chicago Preparatory, Perspectives, Chicago International.

2004
Mayor Daley and CPS announce Renaissance 2010, a plan to create 100 new schools, most of them charter and contract schools, by 2010.

2009
Teachers at the Chicago International Charter School Network sign Chicago's first charter school union contract.

2015
CPS Board of Education votes to close 4 under-performing charter schools. The schools contest the decision to the Illinois State Charter School Commission.

2015
ChiACTS union (Chicago Alliance of Charter Teachers and Staff) represents 1,000 teachers and staff at 32 schools, one-fifth of the city's charters.

2016
3 of the 4 charter schools voted to close by the district win a reprieve from the Illinois State Charter School Commission.

CHAPTER 1

A Brief History of Charter Schools in CPS

Charter legislation was first passed in Illinois in 1996, and six charter schools opened in CPS during the following year (**see Figure 1** for a timeline highlighting key points in CPS charter school history). Enrollments in these schools remained low through the early 2000s (**see Figure 2**), but in 2004, CPS and the City of Chicago jointly launched Renaissance 2010, which called for the creation of 100 new schools by 2010. This initiative increased the pace at which new charter schools were opened in the district, and enrollment grew steadily. By 2016, charter enrollments comprised 11 percent of total enrollments in grades K-8 and 22 percent of total enrollments in grades 9–12. There was a total of 52 elementary charter schools, 34 charter high schools, and 13 charter combination schools (combination schools include both elementary and high school grades) that year.

CPS serves as one of two authorizing agencies for charter schools in the city, meaning it approves or denies applications for new charter schools and renewals for existing charter schools. The Illinois State Charter School Commission is also an authorizing agency for charter schools in Chicago, and throughout the State of Illinois. Founded in 2011, the Commission reviews appeals of charter school proposals and renewal applications that have been denied or revoked by a local school board in Illinois. It can make independent decisions to authorize new applications or renewals or overturn decisions made by a local school board to close a charter school.[24] (**See "Tensions Around Charter Schools in CPS" on p.14 for additional details about the Commission's role in CPS.**)

Each year, CPS releases a Request for Proposals (RFP), soliciting proposals for new charter schools.

FIGURE 2

Enrollment in CPS Charter Schools Has Increased Substantially in the Last 10 Years

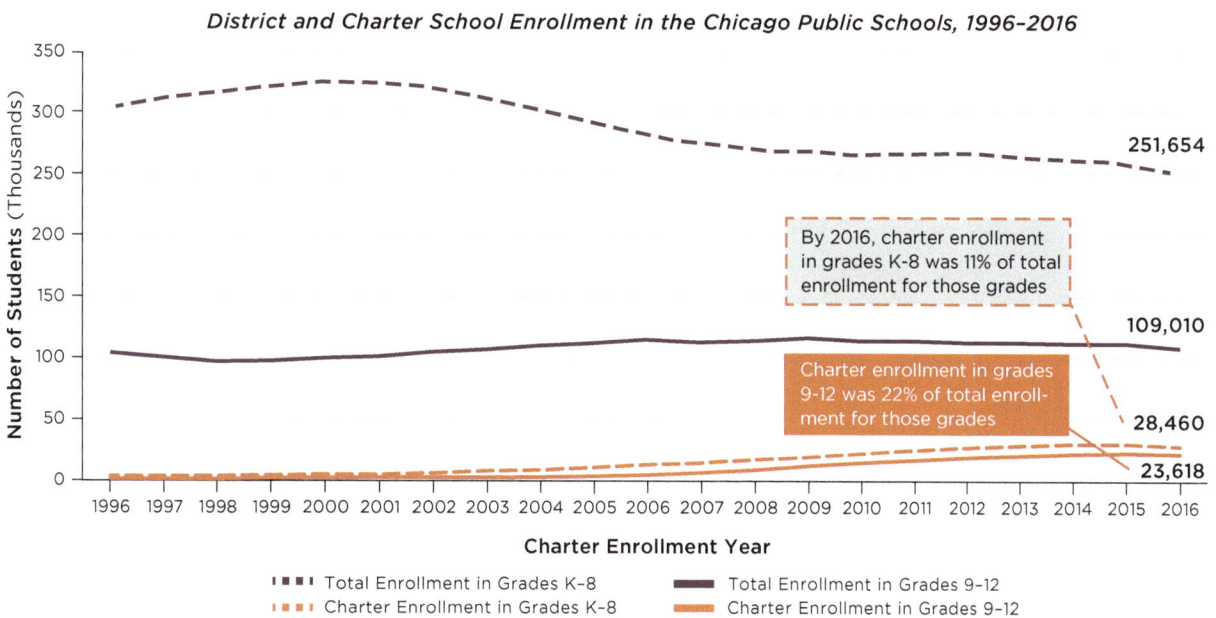

District and Charter School Enrollment in the Chicago Public Schools, 1996–2016

By 2016, charter enrollment in grades K-8 was 11% of total enrollment for those grades

Charter enrollment in grades 9-12 was 22% of total enrollment for those grades

251,654
109,010
28,460
23,618

Number of Students (Thousands)

Charter Enrollment Year

I▪I▪I Total Enrollment in Grades K–8
I▪I▪I Charter Enrollment in Grades K–8
▬▬ Total Enrollment in Grades 9–12
▬▬ Charter Enrollment in Grades 9–12

Note: Total enrollment numbers for K–8 and 9–12 include students who were enrolled in charter schools at each of those grade levels.

24 Illinois State Charter School Commission (2015).

RFPs often prioritize specific areas of the city where the district would like to see new schools located, typically because existing schools are either over-enrolled or because the district has identified a need for improved education outcomes.[25] These are often higher-poverty neighborhoods; as a result of this prioritization, charter high schools are indeed more likely to be located in some of the poorest neighborhoods in Chicago (**see Figure 3**). Proposals are reviewed by a panel of district administrators, and five-year contracts are awarded to organizations whose proposals have been approved by the panel. In making decisions about whether to award a new contract, the district cannot exceed the current cap on the total number of charters allowed in CPS (75 at the time of this report). However, proposals submitted by an existing Charter Management Organization (CMO) are classified as new campuses and do not count against the overall cap. Most new charter campuses during the last several years have been part of existing CMOs rather than free-standing schools.

Charter high schools in Chicago can differ significantly from one another, and also from non-charter schools, in terms of their mission, curriculum, and practices. One of the most obvious ways charter schools differ from non-charter schools and even from one another, is in their management structure. Of the 47 charter schools serving high school students in 2016, five were free-standing charters and the remaining 42 high schools were either part of a CMO or an education management organization (EMO). The largest CMO for high schools is The Noble Network, which, as of 2016, had 17 high school campuses (**see Table 1 on p.16**).

While CMOs are generally non-profit or not-for-profit, EMOs are typically for-profit organizations. Both kinds of organizations oversee a range of administrative responsibilities for the schools they serve, although this can vary substantially from one group to another. In some cases, the management organization establishes the curriculum, discipline policies, after-school offerings, and other policies so that there is consistency in these areas across all schools within the group. In other instances, individual campuses are run autonomously, with school leaders making decisions about these areas. As a result, each individual school campus can be very different from other campuses, even within the same management group.

In interviews, charter leaders highlighted the challenge of balancing autonomy and consistency across charter campuses. One CMO leader described concerns about too much consistency: *"To build a system that works for all of our campuses can inhibit growth."* Another charter high school principal described the tension of wanting autonomy as a school leader, but also support from the CMO: *"It's a tricky balance—how much support would they provide us as a campus with still being able to preserve my autonomy as a principal or our autonomy as a staff to be able to do what we need to do, right?"* In general, CMO leadership tends to view their role as supportive, intentionally not wanting to replicate CPS's *"central office"* and, instead, avoid bureaucracy. As one CMO leader said, *"We are not the central office. We are the support hub and we try to operate in that manner."* Another described their decision to provide individual school principals autonomy: *"We believe that people closest to kids will make the best decisions about them if you give them the opportunity to do it. I think what underpins this organizational intention is to not have a lot of bureaucracy."*

Tensions Around Charter Schools in CPS

The expansion of charter schools in CPS has been a contentious issue for a number of reasons. Illinois Governor Bruce Rauner and Chicago Mayor Rahm Emanuel have shown strong support for the city's charter schools, pointing to large test score gains among many of these schools; however, critics of charter schools are skeptical that these gains are real and question the practices of many charter schools around enrollment and retention.[26] Tensions around growing charter enrollments have been compounded with the district's adoption of student-based budgeting practices, which means that funding is allocated to schools based on the number of

---

25 See http://cps.edu/NewSchools/Pages/RFP2017.aspx for a description of the process for opening new charter schools.

26 Joravsky (2013, December 31); Chicago Tribune (2014, February 27).

FIGURE 3

Most Charter High Schools in CPS Are Located in Neighborhoods with the Highest Concentrations of Poverty

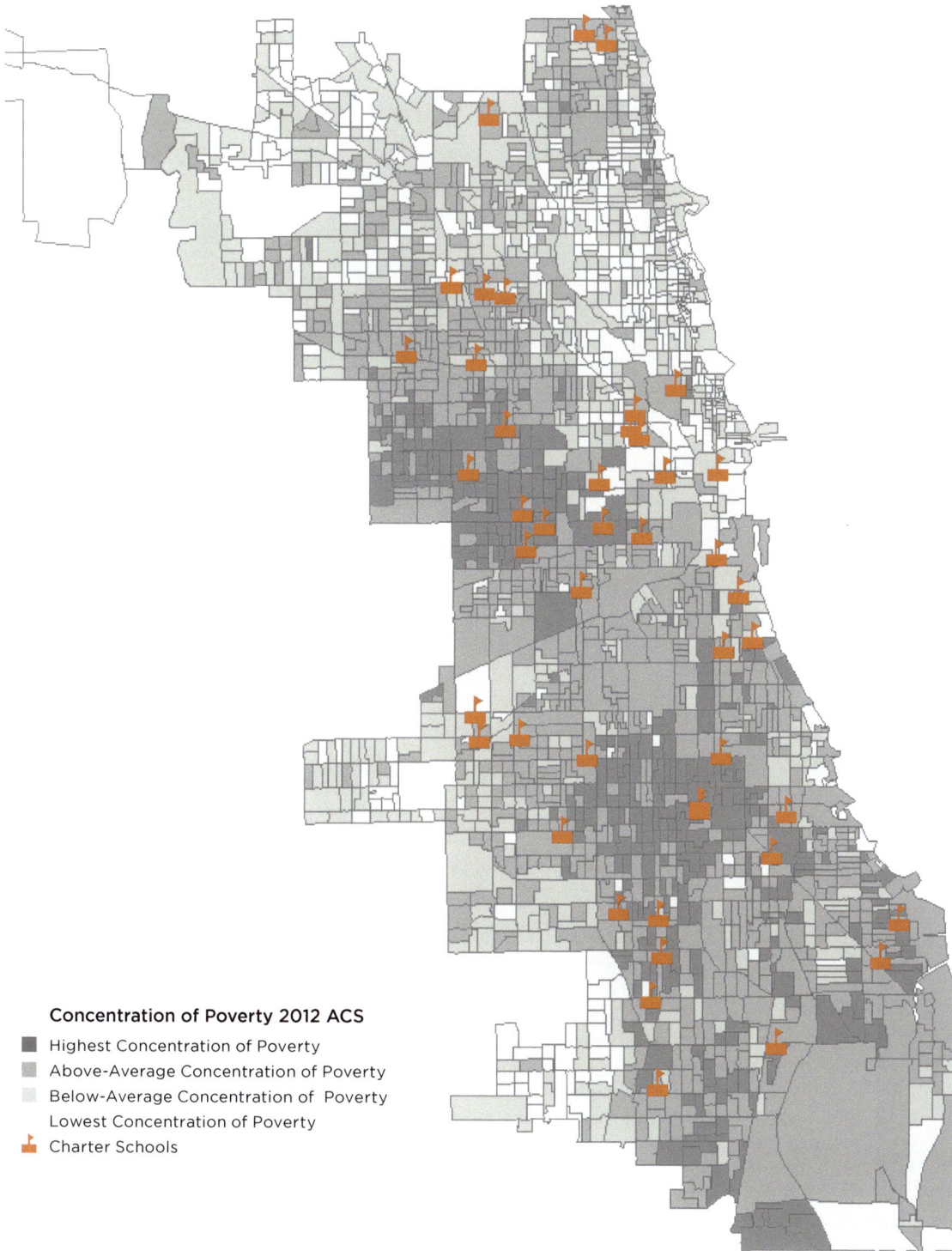

Concentration of Poverty 2012 ACS

- Highest Concentration of Poverty
- Above-Average Concentration of Poverty
- Below-Average Concentration of Poverty
- Lowest Concentration of Poverty
- Charter Schools

Notes: This map shows the location of charter high schools that were open during the 2016–17 school year and served at least one high school grade (grades 9–12). The level of concentrated poverty was calculated for each neighborhood census block using two indicators from the American Community Survey 5 Year Data from 2012: the percent of adult males who are unemployed in the tract and the percent of families with incomes below the poverty line. Highest-poverty census blocks are those with a concentration of poverty that was 1 standard deviation or higher above the average level. Above-average poverty census blocks had poverty concentrations between 0 and 0.99 standard deviations, and below-average poverty census blocks are those with a poverty concentration level between -0.99 and 0 standard deviations. Lowest-poverty census blocks are those with a concentration of poverty that is less than -1 standard deviation.

TABLE 1

Most Charter High Schools in CPS Are Part of a Charter Management Organization (CMO)

Charter Management Organization (CMO)	Education Management Organization (EMO)	Stand Alone
ASPIRA–Business and Finance	Chicago Virtual	Architecture, Construction and Engineering (ACE) Technical
ASPIRA–Early College		EPIC Academy
Catalyst–Maria		Foundations College Prep
Chicago Math & Science Academy[1]		Legal Prep Academy
Horizon Science–McKinley Park[1]		
Instituto Health Sciences Career Academy		Young Women's Leadership
Intrinsic		
Chicago International–Chicago Quest[2]		
Chicago International–Ellison[2]		
Chicago International–Longwood[2]		
Chicago International–Northtown[2]		
Noble Street College Prep		
Noble–The Noble Academy		
Noble–Baker College Prep		
Noble–Chicago Bulls College Prep		
Noble–Butler College Prep		
Noble–Gary Comer College Prep		
Noble–DRW College Prep		
Noble–Golder College Prep		
Noble–Hansberry College Prep		
Noble–ITW David Speer Academy		
Noble–Johnson High School		
Noble–Mansueto		
Noble–Muchin College Prep		
Noble–Pritzker College Prep		
Noble–Rauner College Prep		
Noble–Rowe Clark Math & Science Academy		
Noble–UIC College Prep		
North Lawndale College Prep-Christiana		
North Lawndale College Prep-Collins		
Perspectives–Rodney D Joslin		
Perspectives Leadership Academy		
Perspectives–IIT Math & Science Academy		
Perspectives High School of Technology		
UNO–Major Hector P. Garcia MD		
UNO–Soccer Academy		
UNO–Rogers Park		
University of Chicago–Woodlawn		
Urban Prep–Bronzville		
Urban Prep–Englewood		
Urban Prep–West		

Notes: This table includes charter schools that were open during the 2016-17 school year and served at least one high school grade (grades 9–12).

[1] Chicago Math and Science Academy and Horizon Science are operated by a third-party operator, Concept Schools.

[2] CICS schools are operated by several different third-party-operator CMOs. Chicago Quest, Ellison, and Northtown are all operated by Civitas Education Partners and Longwood is run by Charter Schools USA

students who are enrolled as of the 20th day of school. Over the last decade, many non-charter schools have experienced declines in enrollments resulting in substantially smaller budgets. Declining enrollments and budgets can mean that schools are at greater risk of being closed.

The role of the Illinois State Charter School Commission (SCSC) has also added to tensions surrounding charter schools in CPS. Founded in 2011, this body can make independent decisions about applications for new charters and renewals of existing charter schools. This can create tension with the district, since the SCSC has the authority to grant a contract to an organization whose proposal for a new school was not accepted by the district. When this occurs, funding for this new school or campus does not flow through the district but, instead, comes directly from state funds; ultimately, this can mean a loss of money for the district.[27] The SCSC also has the authority to overrule district decisions about charter renewals. For example, in March 2016, the SCSC voted to overrule a decision made by the district to close three charter schools at the end of the academic year because it felt that the city had not complied with the terms of the charter agreements.[28] The district responded by suing the SCSC on the grounds that it "acted beyond its statutory authority."[29]

The Chicago Teachers Union (CTU) has been a vocal critic of charter schools, particularly as it has watched neighborhood schools struggle with smaller budgets and declining enrollments. Curbing the growth of charter schools is a priority of the CTU, and this became part of contract negotiations between the CTU and CPS in 2016. An agreement was reached that the number of charter schools in the district would not increase for the next five years.[30] For their part, charter schools have sometimes been seen as being anti-union, but in 2017, teachers from one of the largest networks of charters schools in CPS announced plans to unionize. Several other charter schools in CPS had already established teacher unions, although these unions are separate from the CTU.[31]

Finally, there is a widespread perception that charter schools in Chicago receive considerable financial support from private sources, which allows them to build better facilities and provide more resources to their schools and students. Understandably, this creates tensions with non-charter schools, given their own budget constraints. It is worth noting, however, that private support for charter schools is also subject to some uncertainty. In 2016, one of the largest private donors to charter schools in Chicago withdrew much of its support due to its own financial issues, and also because of public backlash towards the city's charter schools.[32]

The next chapter examines some of the policies and practices of charter high schools, including the number of instructional days they offered and their requirements for grade-level promotion and high school graduation. Using the five essential supports framework, we also compare charter high schools to non-charter high schools in terms of their organizational capacity, including effective leadership, collaborative teachers, involved families, supportive environment, and ambitious instruction.

---

27 The district uses a portion of the per-pupil funds received from the state to provide centralized services for all schools, (e.g., trainings; supports for compliance). When charter schools receive per-pupil funding directly from the state, the portion that typically goes to the district for centralized supports flows directly to charter schools.

28 Friedman (2016, March 2).
29 Perez (2016, March 1); Perez (2016, March 23).
30 Fitzpatrick (2016, October 17).
31 Fitzpatrick (2017, March 3).
32 Sanchez (2016, April 22).

CHAPTER 2

Organizational Capacity and Practices

When charter schools first appeared as part of the educational landscape in the early 1990s, they did so with the promise of serving as laboratories of innovation, potentially rethinking every aspect of schooling from the length of the school year to the instructional practices used in the classroom. But how different are charters schools from traditional public schools? To answer this question, we first reviewed some of the policies and practices that charter schools have adopted to support student achievement. We then examined the organizational capacity of CPS charter high schools. Building on previous research by Bryk, Sebring, Allensworth, Luppescu, and Easton (2010) that identified five essential organizational supports necessary for school success, we examined how charter high schools compared to non-charter, non-selective high schools across the following areas: effective leadership, collaborative teachers, involved families, supportive environment, and ambitious instruction.

Charter School Policies and Practices

Most charter high schools had similar numbers of instructional days to CPS. As **Figure 4** shows, CPS had 177 student attendance days in the 2014–15 school year (days in which students were in school). During the same year, 31 charter high schools had between 177 and 180 instructional days. Five charter high schools had 187 or more student attendance days, equivalent to an additional two weeks of school. A small number—six charter high schools—required at least a week less of school than what the district required for non-charter schools.

Most charter schools also had more requirements for promotion to tenth grade than non-charter schools in CPS. CPS required that students pass at least three of their core subject courses in each ninth-grade semester and earn a total of five full-year course credits. Charter schools with more stringent promotion policies required seven to eight full-year course credits and also had additional promotion requirements, including

FIGURE 4

Most CPS Charter High Schools Had a Similar Number of Instructional Days as Non-Charter Schools

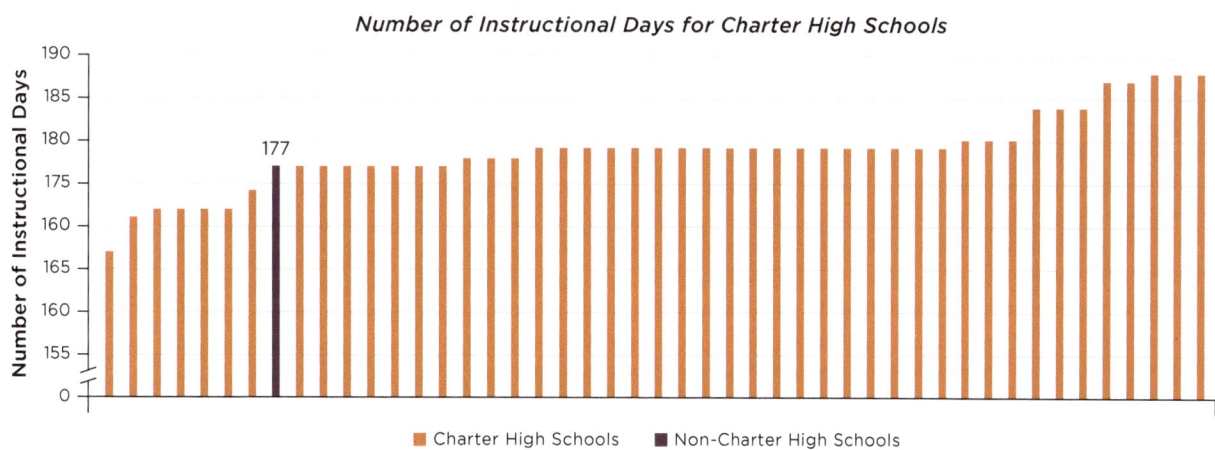

Number of Instructional Days for Charter High Schools

Note: The number of instructional days for charter high schools comes from the 2014-15 school year. This information only includes student attendance days; teacher professional development days, report card pick-up days, and any other non-instructional days were not included. Forty-six charter schools are represented by the orange bars; one charter school that closed at the end of the 2014-15 school year was not included. The purple bar represents the number of instructional days for non-charter CPS schools.

community service (beyond the CPS service learning requirement) or discipline requirements. Others required a C average in order to pass a class. The most stringent charter school required that students pass all classes for promotion to tenth grade.

Charter schools also had more requirements for high school graduation than non-charter high schools. CPS graduation requirements included a minimum of 24 credits and two service learning projects. Some charters required more than 24 credits, with most of these schools requiring 27 to 28 credits, and a few requiring up to 36 credits.[33]

Organizational Capacity and Practices of Charter Schools

Although the policies and practices that schools adopt can have an impact on student learning, the ways in which schools are organized are also critical to their success in educating students. Bryk et al. (2010) identified five key areas of practice, the five essential supports, which are associated with improvements in student learning. These are: effective leaders, collaborative teachers, involved families, a supportive environment, and ambitious instruction. Underlying each of these five dimensions is the notion that the way that teachers, principals, and administrators interact and work with one another, and with students and their families, is critical for promoting strong instruction and student achievement.[34]

The research showed that these five essential supports do not operate in isolation but rather work in concert with one another to lay the foundation for school success. The original study, conducted in elementary schools, showed that schools that are strong in at least three areas are 10 times more likely to show sustained improvement in student achievement than schools that are weak in three or more areas.[35] The strength of

this research has led CPS and many other schools and districts around the country to assess their organizational capacity across these five supports using annual surveys of students and teachers.[36]

Effective Leaders and Collaborative Teachers

One of the most critical components of any school is its leadership. In fact, research has shown successful schools are almost always led by highly *effective leaders*, who ensure there is a clear vision for school improvement.[37] Effective leaders work to establish high standards for teaching and learning and ensure that programs are coordinated and consistent with their goals. They also have a high degree of trust in their staff, whom they empower to participate in a broad range of decisions about policies and practices. Teachers also play a critical role in creating effective schools.[38] *Strong collaboration among teachers* is particularly important as teachers work together to promote professional growth and improve student learning. Equally important is a high level of commitment to the school and a strong degree of trust among teaching staff.

Figure 5 shows how different charter schools were from non-charter, non-selective schools on a number of survey measures describing effective leadership and collaborative teachers. Survey measures were standardized across all four survey years and responses were then aggregated to the school level. Using descriptive statistics, we compared how different charter schools were from non-charter, non-selective schools. Differences are color-coded depending on their magnitude: Measures for which there were no significant differences between charter schools and non-charter, non-selective schools are gray in color. Measures for which charter schools had significantly higher scores

---

33 In the case of schools that require 36 credits, the credits may not exactly correspond to CPS's definition of one credit, which is typically one year-long course

34 Bryk et al. (2010).

35 In more recent years, researchers have also determined that the five essential supports are associated with positive student outcomes in high schools (Sebastian & Allensworth, 2013; Klugman, Gordon, Sebring, & Sporte, 2015).

36 CPS administers the *My Voice, My School* survey each year to all teachers and to students in grades 6–12. Rasch analysis is

used to combine responses on individual items into measures capturing different components of each essential support. UChicago Impact, a partner of the UChicago Consortium, administers the 5Essentials surveys throughout Illinois and in other states, which includes the same set of questions as the *My Voice, My School* survey. See https://www.uchicagoimpact.org/tools-training/5essentials.

37 Leithwood, Louis, Anderson, & Wahlstrom (2004).

38 Bryk at al. (2010); McLaughlin & Talbert (2006); Louis, Marks & Kruse (1996).

than non-charter, non-selective schools are shaded orange, with darker shades indicating increasingly larger differences. Measures on which charter schools had significantly lower scores are shaded purple, with darker shades indicating increasingly larger differences.

Charter school teachers described school leaders in very similar terms as teachers in non-charter, non-selective schools in all four survey years: charter school teachers reported comparable levels of trust in their leaders in three out of four years, and they described school leaders as being equally willing to let teachers influence policies and practices at their schools. Charter school teachers also described their principals as setting similarly high standards for teaching and student learning and they reported similar levels of program coherence as teachers in non-charter, non-selective schools.

FIGURE 5

CPS Charter High School Teachers Described Their School Leaders in Similar Ways as CPS Teachers in Non-Charter, Non-Selective Schools

	Student (S) or Teacher (T) Survey	2011	2012	2013	2014
Effective Leaders					
Teacher-Principal Trust Teachers and principals share high level of mutual trust and respect.	T	0.03	0.04	0.18*	0.05
Teacher Influence Teachers have influence in a broad range of decisions regarding school policies and practices.	T	0.03	0.06	0.08	-0.10
Instructional Leadership The school leadership team sets high standards for teaching and student learning.	T	-0.08	-0.13	0.03	-0.08
Program Coherence School programs are coordinated and consistent with their goals for student learning.	T	0.08	0.03	0.08	-0.08
Collaborative Teachers					
Teacher-Teacher Trust Teachers are supportive and respectful of one another, personally and professionally.	T	0.21***	0.25***	0.15*	0.15*
Collective Responsibility Teachers share a strong sense of responsibility for student development, school improvement and professional growth.	T	0.28***	0.33***	0.28**	0.16*
Collaborative Practices Teachers observe each others' practice and work together to review assessment data and develop instructional strategies.	T	0.12**	0.12	0.11	0.05
Quality Professional Development Professional development is rigorous and focused on student learning.	T	-0.03	-0.02	0.02	-0.10
School Commitment Teachers are deeply committed to the school.	T	-0.08	-0.14	-0.06	-0.22**

≤ -0.21 Standard Deviations	-0.20 to -0.11 Standard Deviations	-0.10 to 0.00 Standard Deviations	No Significant Difference	0.00 to 0.10 Standard Deviations	0.11 to 0.20 Standard Deviations	≥ 0.21 Standard Deviations

Notes: This figure shows average differences of charter schools compared to non-charter schools on each measure of essential support for each year. Measure scores were standardized across all four years and then aggregated to the school level for each year. Descriptive statistics were used to compare the average score of charter schools to non-charter, non-selective schools for each measure in each year. Differences between charter schools and non-charter, non-selective schools are color-coded based on their magnitude: Measures for which there are no significant differences are gray in color. Measures for which charter schools had significantly higher scores than non-charter, non-selective schools are shaded orange, with darker shades indicating increasingly larger differences. Measures on which charter schools had significantly lower scores are shaded purple, with darker shades indicating increasingly larger differences. * indicates that differences are significant at $p<0.05$; ** indicates that differences are significant at $p<0.01$ and *** indicates that differences are significant at $p<0.001$.

Despite similar reports about school leaders, charter school teachers differed from teachers in non-charter, non-selective schools in reports about interactions with colleagues on some dimensions. Charter school teachers described their relationships with colleagues as characterized by higher levels of trust, compared to teachers in non-charter, non-selective schools, and they also described colleagues as having a stronger sense of responsibility for student development, school improvement, and professional growth. That being said, charter school teachers were no more likely than teachers in non-charter schools to collaborate with colleagues to improve their practice, at least in 2012, 2013, and 2014.

In terms of professional learning opportunities, charter school teachers described their professional development as being of similar quality, compared to teachers in non-charter, non-selective schools. Charter school teachers reported somewhat lower levels of school commitment in 2011, 2012, and 2013, and significantly lower levels in 2014.[39]

For most measures describing effective leaders and collaborative teachers, there was a trend in which charter differences in 2013 and 2014 were either smaller than previous years or negative when previous years were positive. Were charter schools' scores on these measures going down in 2013 and 2014 or were scores for non-charter, non-selective schools going up? In general, smaller differences in 2013 and 2014 were due to increases in scores for non-charter, non-selective schools rather than decreases in scores for charter schools. This pattern is also evident for other measures of essential supports, as **Figure 6** and **Figure 8** show.

Involved Families and Supportive Environments

Beyond relationships that school staff have with one another, close connections with families are also important for supporting a strong learning environment.

Strong family–school ties can mean parents are able to reinforce learning at home and schools can benefit from parental input about their children. Given that charter school families have actively chosen to enroll their students in these schools, it's not altogether surprising that they might have stronger relationships with the school. **Figure 6** shows that charter school teachers reported significantly higher levels of parental involvement across all four years and greater levels of trust with the parent community, through 2013, compared to teachers in non-charter, non-selective schools. Nevertheless, having a more involved parent body does not mean parents have more influence over decision making in charter schools. In fact, teachers reported that parents had significantly less influence on school policies and practices in charter schools than in non-charter, non-selective schools.

The *school environment* also plays an important role in establishing a strong foundation for learning. A safe climate is particularly critical for student success. Students who feel unsafe at their school or whose school day is disrupted by frequent altercations are unlikely to learn at their fullest capacity. Supportive relationships with teachers are also foundational for student success, as are the expectations that school staff hold for their students and for their future educational attainment.

Charter school teachers and students offered more positive accounts of their school environments than students and teachers in non-charter, non-selective schools. For example, charter school students reported feeling significantly safer at school in 2011, 2012, and 2013.[40] They also described their relationships with teachers in 2011 and 2012 as more trusting. In 2013 and 2014, the level of trust reported by students in non-charter, non-selective schools increased, so that the differences between these schools and charter schools were smaller than in previous years.

Increases in the level of student-teacher trust in recent years may mean that non-charter schools were

---

39 Prior Consortium research has shown that schools in which teachers report lower levels of school commitment have higher rates of teacher turnover, on average (Allensworth, Ponisciak, & Mazzeo, 2009). Although this report does not address the issue of teacher retention, research has shown that charter school teachers are more likely to leave their school and they are more likely to leave the teaching profession altogether (Renzulli, Parrott, & Beattie, 2011).

40 The safety measure included items that asked how safe students felt in their school and also items about how safe students felt outside of their school. The neighborhoods in which high schools are located can be an important factor in how safe students feel outside of their school, and these conditions are not always within the ability of the school to control.

actively working on improving relationships between students and teachers. In charter schools, a focus on the whole student and strong connections between students and school staff members were seen by school leaders as one of their greatest strengths. One charter school leader described how they allocated time during the school day to build relationships: *"We have daily time set aside where students are able to greet one another, give a hug, or acknowledge a student who is showing resilience overcoming an issue from the previous day or week. These instances of being intentional about positivity and love are important."*

Another charter school leader described the importance of building in structures so staff members can connect with one another: *"There's a strong emphasis here on the social emotional well-being of our staff and our students. We have these points every week where we stop everything and then the adults can learn from one another, and we are really intentional about that scheduling."*

Figure 6 also shows that charter school students described their schools as more likely to engage students in planning for their life after high school graduation. This aligns with charter school teachers' reports that their schools were more likely to expect all students to attend college and promote college readiness than non-charter, non-selective schools. The size of the difference in charter teachers' reports is particularly noteworthy. In 2011–13, charter teachers' scores were around one-half a standard deviation higher on this measure than teachers in non-charter, non-selective schools, a sizeable difference.

FIGURE 6

CPS Charter High School Teachers and Students Described Having More Involved Families and More Supportive Communities at Their Schools than CPS Teachers in Non-Charter, Non-Selective Schools

	Student (S) or Teacher (T) Survey	2011	2012	2013	2014
Involved Families					
Teacher-Parent Trust Teachers and parents are partners in improving student learning.	T	0.27***	0.21**	0.27**	0.12
Parent Involvement in School Parents are active participants in their child's schooling.	T	N/A	0.35***	0.33***	0.19**
Parent Influence on Decision-Making The school has created opportunities for parents to participate in developing academic programs and influencing school curricula.	T	N/A	N/A	N/A	-0.40***
Supportive Environment					
Safety Students feel safe in and around school.	S	0.18**	0.12*	0.11*	0.08
School-Wide Future Orientation The school engages all students in planning for life after graduation.	S	0.28***	0.32***	0.27***	0.19***
Student-Teacher Trust Students and teachers share a high level of mutual trust and respect.	S	0.12**	0.08*	0.07	0.04
Expectations for Postsecondary Education The school expects all students to attend college and promotes college readiness.	T	0.56***	0.45***	0.55***	0.32***

≤ -0.21 Standard Deviations	-0.20 to -0.11 Standard Deviations	-0.10 to 0.00 Standard Deviations	No Significant Difference	0.00 to 0.10 Standard Deviations	0.11 to 0.20 Standard Deviations	≥ 0.21 Standard Deviations

Notes: This figure shows average differences of charter schools compared to non-charter schools on each measure of essential support for each year. Measure scores were standardized across all four years and then aggregated to the school level for each year. Descriptive statistics were used to compare the average score of charter schools to non-charter, non-selective schools for each measure in each year. Differences between charter schools and non-charter, non-selective schools are color-coded based on their magnitude: measures for which there are no significant differences are gray in color. Measures for which charter schools had significantly higher scores than non-charter, non-selective schools are shaded orange, with darker shades indicating increasingly larger differences. Measures on which charter schools had significantly lower scores are shaded purple, with darker shades indicating increasingly larger differences. * indicates that differences are significant at p<0.05; ** indicates that differences are significant at p<0.01 and *** indicates that differences are significant at p<0.001.

It's possible that charter school students differed from non-charter school students in ways that meant they were more attuned to school staff's efforts to prepare them for post-secondary opportunities, compared to other students. To test this, we compared responses on the school-wide future orientation measure of ninth-grade charter school students in our analytic sample to ninth-grade students enrolled in non-charter high schools, controlling for differences in incoming skills, school experiences, and background characteristics (see Appendix A for details).

The first column in Figure 7 shows the overall charter difference in ninth-grade students' reports about their schools' school-wide future orientation across all four years of survey administration without adjusting for differences between students. Similar to the findings in Figure 6, which includes students in grades 9–12, ninth-grade charter school students were more likely than students in non-charter schools to say their schools engaged everyone in planning for the future. After taking into account differences in incoming skills, experiences, and background characteristics, charter school students were still significantly more likely to describe their schools in this way than students enrolled in non-charter schools.

A strong focus on post-secondary attainment was also identified by charter leaders as one of the strengths of charter schools. During interviews, leaders described how they established college expectations beginning in ninth grade and some described providing support through college graduation. Others described hiring college counselors at each of their campuses to help create a college-going culture at their schools. One charter leader shared: *"I think the other piece that sets us apart is that since our infancy, there's always been a very clear vision for where we are going and what our goal is for kids— the goal is to get our kids to graduate from college."*

Ambitious Instruction

Although charter schools were intended to be laboratories of innovation, it's unclear how much innovation actually occurs in these schools, particularly in terms of instructional practices, which are likely to have the greatest influence on shaping student achievement. The *My Voice, My School* survey asked teachers how willing they were try out innovative practices to improve their teaching. Figure 8 shows that charter school teachers reported greater willingness to try out innovative strategies, compared to teachers in non-charter, non-

FIGURE 7

CPS Ninth-Grade Charter School Students Were More Likely to Say Their Schools Prepared Them for Life After Graduation than Similar Students in Non-Charter High Schools

Differences in Ninth-Grade Charter Students' Reports about School-wide Future Orientation

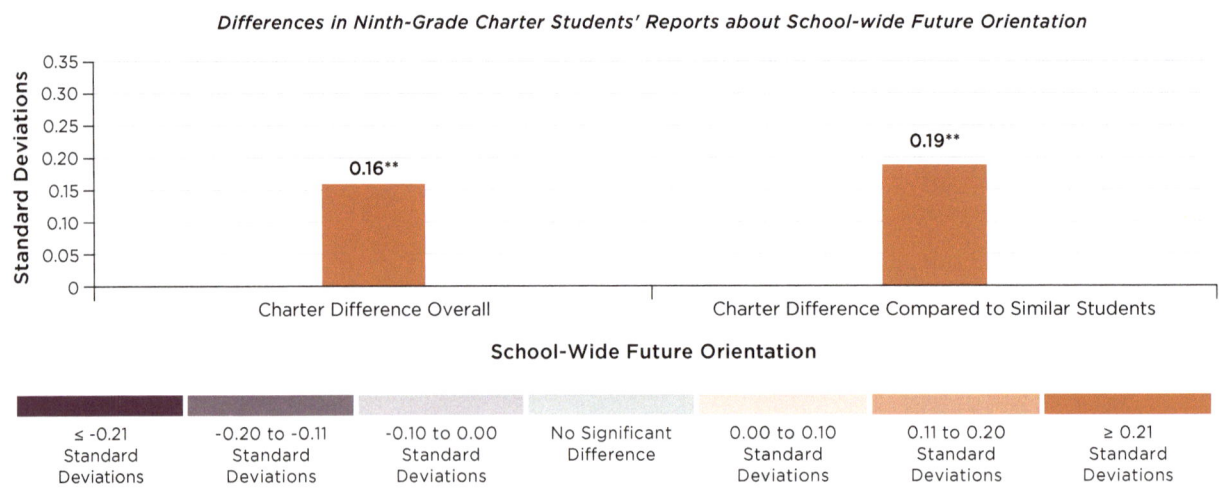

Note: Analyses of differences in reports about School-wide Future Orientation between charter high school students and students in non-charter high schools included first-time ninth-graders in 2010–13. Analyses were conducted using a 2-level HLM model in which students were nested in their ninth-grade schools. Models controlled for an array of eighth-grade academic performance indicators, eighth-grade school experiences, and background characteristics. Control variables were grand-mean centered so that the intercept represents students with typical eighth-grade academic performance, school experiences, and background characteristics who enrolled in a non-charter high school. ** indicates that charter school students had significantly different scores at p<0.01.

selective schools in 2011, 2012, and 2013. However, charter school teachers also described their assignments as having less emphasis on critical thinking, at least in 2014, than teachers in non-charter, non-selective schools. Charter school and non-charter school teachers offered similar reports about how frequently they gave writing assignments and about the quality of student discussion in their classes.[41]

Charter school students offered a somewhat different perspective on their instructional experiences than charter school teachers. In general, they described instruction as more demanding than students in non-charter, non-selective schools did. For example, they were more likely to say that their teachers expected them to do their best and meet academic demands than students in non-charter, non-selective schools (see Figure 8). They

FIGURE 8

CPS Charter High School Students Described Their Schools as Being More Academically Demanding than Students in Non-Charter, Non-Selective Schools

Ambitious Instruction	Student (S) or Teacher (T) Survey	2011	2012	2013	2014
Innovation Teachers are willing to try new ideas to improve their teaching.	T	0.21***	0.24*	0.17*	N/A
Emphasis on Critical Thinking Teachers regularly give assignments requiring students to demonstrate original ideas and use evidence to support these ideas.	T	0.05**	0.03	0.02	-0.08*
Writing Frequency Teachers regularly give assignments requiring students to write and revise multiple pages.	T	0.00	0.01	0.03	-0.03
Quality of Student Discussion Students participate in classroom discussions that build their critical thinking skills.	T	0.07	0.01	0.04	-0.08
Academic Press Teachers expect students to do their best and to meet academic demands.	S	0.19***	0.20***	0.17***	0.14***
English Instruction Students interact with course material and one another to build and apply critical reading and writing skills.	S	0.12***	0.12**	0.08**	0.04
Math Instruction Students interact with course material and one another to build and apply knowledge in their math classes.	S	0.18***	0.24***	0.20***	0.15***

≤ -0.21 Standard Deviations	-0.20 to -0.11 Standard Deviations	-0.10 to 0.00 Standard Deviations	No Significant Difference	0.00 to 0.10 Standard Deviations	0.11 to 0.20 Standard Deviations	≥ 0.21 Standard Deviations

Notes: This figure shows average differences of charter schools compared to non-charter schools on each measure of essential support for each year. Measure scores were standardized across all four years and then aggregated to the school level for each year. Descriptive statistics were used to compare the average score of charter schools to non-charter, non-selective schools for each measure in each year. Differences between charter schools and non-charter, non-selective schools are color-coded based on their magnitude: Measures for which there are no significant differences are gray in color. Measures for which charter schools had significantly higher scores than non-charter, non-selective schools are shaded orange, with darker shades indicating increasingly larger differences. Measures on which charter schools had significantly lower scores are shaded purple, with darker shades indicating increasingly larger differences. * indicates that differences are significant at $p<0.05$; ** indicates that differences are significant at $p<0.01$ and *** indicates that differences are significant at $p<0.001$.

41 The innovation measure was not included on the 2014 survey. The critical thinking and writing frequency measures were removed from the *My Voice, My School* survey after 2014; while on the survey, these measures were auxiliary measures and not included in the five essential supports framework.

were also more likely to say they were engaged in challenging tasks that required critical thinking in their math and English classes than students in other schools.

Again, it's possible that charter students differed from other students in ways that meant they experienced instruction differently. To test this, we compared reports about academic press, English instruction, and math instruction from ninth-grade charter school students in our analytic sample to students in non-charter schools, controlling for differences in incoming skills, school experiences, and background characteristics. For each measure, we first show the overall difference between ninth-grade charter school and non-charter school students in the district, and then we show the difference between charter students and similar students in non-charter schools (**see Figure 9**). Similar to **Figure 8**, ninth-grade charter school students in 2011–14 reported higher levels of academic press and they described their math instruction as being of higher quality compared to non-charter ninth-grade students. Even when we compared charter school students to similar students in the district, charter school students' scores were significantly higher on these measures.

In terms of the quality of English instruction, ninth-grade charter school students' reports were no different, on average, than all other ninth-grade students in the district, nor were they significantly different from students in non-charter schools, once we controlled for differences between students.

Summary

Prior Consortium research identified five organizational supports that are essential for school improvement and student success: effective leadership, collaborative teachers, supportive environment, involved families, and ambitious instruction. Among high schools in Chicago, we found that charter schools were similar to non-charter schools on some dimensions of organizational capacity and different on other dimensions. Charter school teachers described school leaders in much the same way as teachers in non-charter, non-selective schools. In terms of relationships with colleagues, charter school teachers reported higher levels of trust and a greater sense of collective responsibility among teachers in their schools, but their levels of collaboration were, for the most part, similar to teachers in non-charter,

FIGURE 9

CPS Charter High School Ninth-Graders Described Their Classes as More Academically Demanding than Similar Students in Non-Charter, Non-Selective Schools

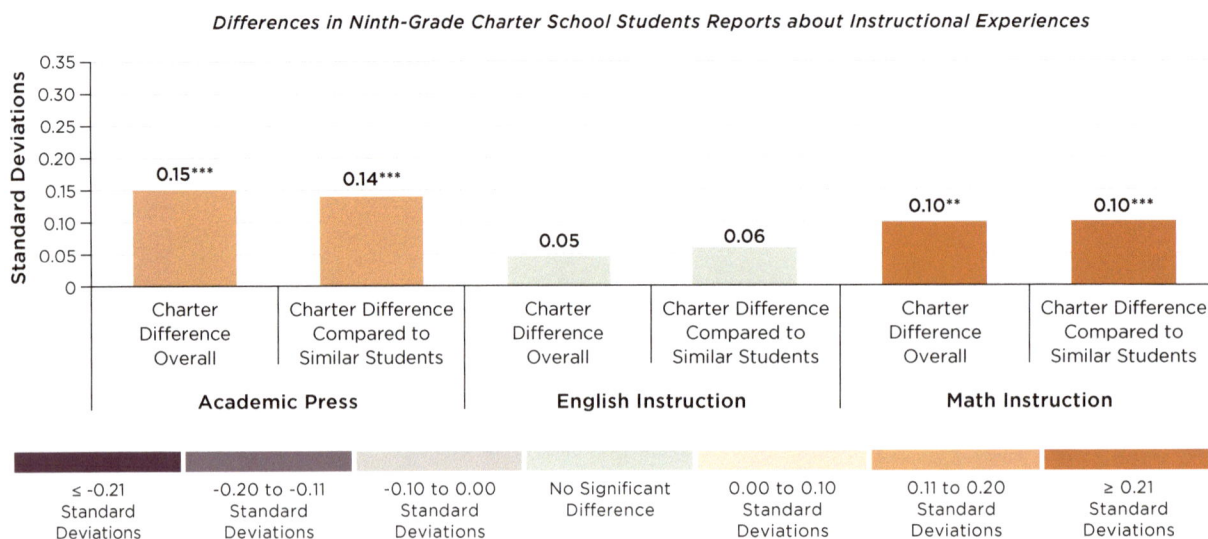

Differences in Ninth-Grade Charter School Students Reports about Instructional Experiences

	Academic Press		English Instruction		Math Instruction	
	Charter Difference Overall	Charter Difference Compared to Similar Students	Charter Difference Overall	Charter Difference Compared to Similar Students	Charter Difference Overall	Charter Difference Compared to Similar Students
Standard Deviations	0.15***	0.14***	0.05	0.06	0.10**	0.10***

Legend:
- ≤ -0.21 Standard Deviations
- -0.20 to -0.11 Standard Deviations
- -0.10 to 0.00 Standard Deviations
- No Significant Difference
- 0.00 to 0.10 Standard Deviations
- 0.11 to 0.20 Standard Deviations
- ≥ 0.21 Standard Deviations

Note: Analyses of differences between charter high school students and students in non-charter high schools in their reports about instructional experiences included first-time ninth-graders in 2010-2013. Analyses were conducted using a 2-level HLM model in which students were nested in their ninth-grade schools. Models controlled for an array of eighth-grade academic performance indicators, eighth-grade school experiences, and background characteristics. Control variables were grand-mean centered so that the intercept represents students with typical eighth-grade academic performance, school experiences, and background characteristics who enrolled in a non-charter high school. ** indicates that charter school students had significantly different scores at $p<0.01$ and *** indicates that charter school students had significantly different scores at $p<0.001$.

non-selective schools. In 2014, charter school teachers reported significantly lower levels of school commitment compared to non-charter, non-selective school teachers.

Charter schools looked most different from non-charter, non-selective schools in their academic preparation of students for the future. Most charter schools had more requirements for grade-level promotion and graduation, although they had a comparable number of instructional days as non-charter schools. Charter school teachers reported greater willingness to try innovative strategies in the classroom, and students in these schools described their classes as being more academically demanding. Charter school students were also more likely to say their schools engaged all students in planning for the future, compared to similar students in non-charter schools. This aligned with reports by charter school teachers, who were more likely to say their schools expected all students to attend college and they promoted college readiness than teachers in non-charter, non-selective high schools.

In the next chapter, we explore who enrolled in charter high schools and whether their incoming qualifications and characteristics differed from students who enrolled in other kinds of high schools.

CHAPTER 3

Incoming Academic Skills and Behaviors

Concerns that charter schools may enroll mostly high-performing students, while leaving behind low-achieving students for traditional public schools, continue to be part of local and national debates about charter schools. This chapter examines the prior academic achievement and behaviors of CPS charter school students to assess whether these students looked systematically different from other students before they entered high school.

An important component in understanding whether charter schools enroll students that are distinctive in terms of prior performance is knowing what other high school options may be available and whether these options select students based on performance. In CPS, charter schools are one of a number of types of schools available to high school students, including neighborhood schools, selective enrollment schools, military schools, magnet schools, career academies, and small schools. Some of these schools have specific criteria for admission based on academic performance. For example, selective enrollment and military schools require a minimum score on an entrance exam, in addition to other criteria. Other schools, including magnet schools and career academies, may also have admission requirements based on test scores, attendance, or grades.[42] Charter schools, however, are prohibited from these kinds of performance requirements for admission. Students who want to attend any school other than their neighborhood school, including charter schools, are required to submit an application, and enrollment may be determined by lottery if applications exceed availability.[43] Only around one-half of all CPS charter high schools run lotteries.[44]

Most students who were first-time ninth-graders in 2010–13 enrolled in a high school other than their assigned neighborhood school: twenty-two percent of students enrolled in charter high schools and 50 percent enrolled in district-run high schools other than their attendance area school (see Figure 10). As shown in Table A, in the box titled "A District-Level Comparison of Students' Incoming Characteristics," there were considerable differences in the incoming skills and behaviors of students who enrolled in different types of high schools. Given the admission requirements that selective enrollment, military, and magnet schools have, it is not surprising that students who enrolled in these schools had the highest average test scores, grades, and

FIGURE 10

Nearly One-Quarter of CPS First-Time Ninth-Graders in 2010–13 Enrolled in Charter High School

High School Choices of First-Time Ninth-Grade Students in 2010–2013

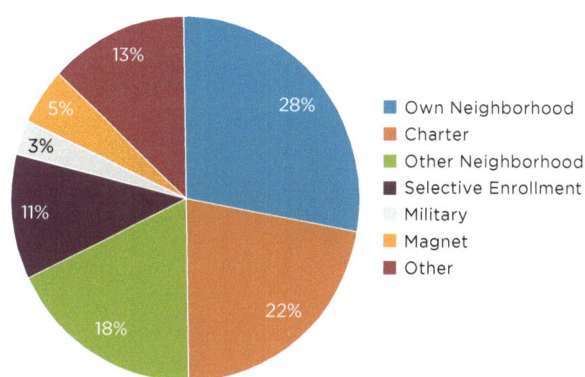

Note: This figure is based on enrollment data for students who were first-time ninth-graders in 2010–13. Other high schools included career academies, small schools, International Baccalaureate schools, and Early College STEM schools.

---

42 Some specialty schools have other requirements for admission. For example, the Chicago High School for the Arts requires live auditions.

43 Beginning in the 2017–18 school year, CPS transitioned to a universal application system for students applying to CPS high schools other than selective enrollment schools. The goal of the new system is to simplify the high school application process and increase transparency and equity in the high school

enrollment process. All district-run schools were required to participate and nearly all charter high schools agreed to participate. See http://go.cps.edu/about/participating-school for a list of participating high schools, including charter high schools.

44 For example, during the 2014-15 school year, 24 out of 47 charter high schools conducted lotteries to determine ninth-grade enrollments.

attendance of any group of students enrolled in other schools. By contrast, charter school students and students who remained in their neighborhood schools had the lowest average test scores.

A district-level comparison of this kind can be useful for providing a high-level overview, but it doesn't take into account the fact that charter schools are more likely to be located in higher-poverty neighborhoods (**see Figure 3**

A District Level Comparison of Students' Incoming Characteristics

Given the range of high school options available to CPS students and the admission requirements at some schools, it's not surprising that there were differences across types of high schools in the incoming characteristics of students. As Table A shows, students who enrolled in selective enrollment high schools, magnet high schools, and military academies had the highest average eighth-grade math scores, attendance, and GPA of any type of school; their scores were also well above the district average. At the other end of the spectrum, students who stayed in their own neighborhood schools had the lowest eighth-grade test scores, GPA, and attendance rates of students in other types of schools.

Charter school students, along with students who remained in their neighborhood schools, had the lowest average test scores. But on a number of other dimensions—including GPA, percent of students with an identified disability, percent who are English Language Learners (ELL), percent who qualify for free lunch, and average distance travelled to school—charter students looked more similar to students who opted out of their assigned neighborhood school in favor of another neighborhood school. In terms of their eighth-grade attendance, charter school students were similar to students who enrolled in higher performing schools, including magnet schools and military academies.

TABLE A

Charter School Students Entered High School with Some of the Lowest Average Test Scores of Any Group of Students Attending Other CPS High Schools

Type of High School	Avg. 8th-Grade Math Test Scores	Avg. 8th-Grade GPA	Avg. 8th-Grade Attend. Rate	8th-Grade Sp. Ed	8th-Grade ELL	8th-Grade Free Lunch	Black	Latino	Avg. Distance to School
District Average (SD)	267.7 (23.7)	2.62 (0.82)	94.6% (6.4%)	15.4%	7.2%	83.2%	43.3%	44.1%	2.8 miles
Own Neighborhood High School	261.4	2.43	94.1%	18.3%	13.0%	86.4%	26.5%	60.3%	1.3 miles
Charter High School	261.2	2.53	95.3%	17.1%	6.1%	85.2%	57.6%	36.9%	3.1 miles
Career Academy Small School	262.9	2.51	94.3%	16.1%	4.4%	88.6%	66.8%	28.6%	2.7 miles
Other Neighborhood High School	266.4	2.55	93.3%	15.2%	7.1%	85.3%	45.4%	41.9%	3.1 miles
Military Academy	270.5	2.68	95.7%	9.6%	2.7%	86.2%	40.4%	86.2%	4.5 miles
Magnet High School	274.9	2.86	95.7%	11.2%	3.0%	76.3%	32.7%	47.7%	3.0 miles
Selective Enrollment High School	302.6	3.57	96.7%	6.7%	0.4%	60.3%	34.3%	33.6%	4.8 miles

Note: Table A shows the incoming (eighth-grade) skills, academic behaviors, and background characteristics for students who were first-time ninth-graders in 2010–13, by the type of high school in which they enrolled. The "% 8th-Grade Sp. Ed" included any students with an identified disability. We used the percent of students who qualified for free lunch, rather than the more typical free or reduced-price lunch, because it is a better indicator of student disadvantage in a district where most students meet the minimum requirement for reduced lunch.

on p.15), and like most schools, serve students from the surrounding communities.[45] It is possible that charter schools enrolled a greater proportion of higher-achieving students from surrounding communities than other nearby schools and still served students whose achievement level was below the district average. To investigate this possibility, we compared students who enrolled in a given charter school to a *"feeder pool"* of students who lived in the same neighborhood as enrollees or attended the same elementary school, but who did not attend that charter school.[46] (See Appendix A for a description of how we identified the feeder pool for each high school.)

A Feeder Pool Comparison

We used data on students who were first-time ninth-graders in 2013 to analyze how charter school students compared to their feeder pool on eighth-grade indicators, including test scores, study habits, GPA, and attendance. In **Figures 11–14**, each orange diamond represents a charter school that was open during the 2013-14 school year. A school's location on the chart is based on two pieces of information: First, the average score of its enrollees on a given indicator determines the school's location on the horizontal axis. Second, the average score of its feeder pool—students who came from the same neighborhoods and elementary schools as enrollees but enrolled in a different school—determines the school's location on the vertical axis. In general, charter schools that appear to the right of the diagonal line on the chart enrolled students with stronger incoming qualifications than others in their feeder pool. Those on the left enrolled students with weaker qualifications. **See the box titled "How to Read the Figures in This Section"** for more details about these figures.

Figures 11–14 show how enrollees in each charter high school compared to their feeder pools on test scores, study habits, GPA, and attendance. Looking across all four figures, there is a gradual transition of schools from the lower left quadrant in **Figure 11** to the upper right quadrant in **Figure 14**. Most charter schools enrolled students whose test scores were similar to or below the test scores of their feeder pool but whose eighth-grade attendance was higher than their feeder pool. More specifically:

- **Test Scores** (**Figure 11**): Most charter schools enrolled students whose eighth-grade test scores were either below their feeder pool (these schools are located to the left of the dashed horizontal lines) or similar to their feeder pool (these schools fall in between the two diagonal lines). Only four schools had students whose test scores were more than one-tenth of a standard deviation higher than their feeder pool.

- **Study Habits** (**Figure 12**): Using students' responses on CPS's annual *My Voice, My School* survey about how much they prioritize studying,[47] we found that nearly all charter schools had students whose eighth-grade study habits were similar to their feeder pool.

- **GPAs** (**Figure 13**): Around one-third of charter schools had students with GPAs that were lower than their feeder pool, one-third enrolled students whose GPAs were similar to their feeder pool, and one-third enrolled students whose GPAs were higher than their feeder pool.

- **Attendance** (**Figure 14**): Nearly two-thirds of charter high schools enrolled students whose attendance rates were substantially higher than their feeder pool, and around one-third of this group had students whose attendance rates were dramatically higher than their feeder pool (more than three-tenths of a standard deviation). Only a small handful of charter schools enrolled students whose attendance rates were lower, on average, than their feeder pool.[48]

---

45 As Table A shows, students who enrolled in a charter high school travelled an average of 3.1 miles to get to school. While this was farther than the average distance travelled by students who remained in their own neighborhood schools, it was comparable to the average distances travelled by students attending other neighborhood schools outside of their attendance areas and magnet schools, and it was less than the average distance travelled by students who enrolled in military and selective enrollment schools.

46 Students who enrolled in selective enrollment high schools were excluded from the feeder pools because their prior achievement levels were so much higher that they are not reasonably likely to attend a charter school.

47 Incoming study habits of first-time ninth-grade students in

2013 were measured based on their responses to four items on CPS's annual *My Voice, My School* survey, administered in spring 2013, when students were in eighth grade. Students were asked how much they agreed with the following questions: I always study for tests; I set aside time to do my homework and study; I try to do well on my schoolwork even when it isn't interesting to me; if I need to study, I don't go out with friends. Students' responses were combined into a single measure using Rasch analysis and scores on this measure were standardized across all first-time ninth-grade students in 2013.

48 We also compared eighth-grade suspensions of charter school students to students in their feeder pools and found that most charter schools enrolled students with similar rates of suspensions as their feeder pools.

The sample figure shown in Figure A shows how students who enrolled in each charter high school compared to their feeder pool in terms of an eighth-grade indicator—in this case, test scores. Each orange diamond represents a hypothetical charter school. Each charter school's location on the chart is based on two pieces of information: First, a school's location along the horizontal axis describes the average eighth-grade test scores of students who enrolled in that school. Second, its location on the vertical axis describes the average eighth-grade scores of its feeder pool—that is, students who came from the same neighborhoods and elementary schools as its enrollees but who enrolled in different high schools. The "zero" point represents the district average for eighth-grade test scores.

A charter school which enrolled students with average eighth-grade test scores that were the same as its feeder pool can fall at any point along the diagonal line that runs from the bottom left corner to the upper right corner through the center of the chart. The charter school in the upper right quadrant of **Figure A** labeled with "1" is an example of this case. On average, its enrollees had average eighth-grade test scores that were 0.6 standard deviations above the district average and its feeder pool had the same average test scores.

Charter schools that fall to the left of the diagonal line had students with lower test scores, on average, than their feeder pools. For example, the charter school labeled "2" enrolled students whose eighth-grade test scores were typical for the district, but it drew from a feeder pool that, on average, had scores that were well above the district average. By contrast, the charter school labeled "3" enrolled students whose eighth-grade test scores were well below the district average (0.4 standard deviations below), but the test scores of the feeder pool were slightly above the district average.

Charter schools that fall to the right of the diagonal enrolled students with higher scores, on average, than their feeder pools. The two charter schools labeled "4" and "5" both had students whose eighth-grade test scores were higher than their feeder pool, but the charter school labeled "5" enrolled students whose test scores were close to the district average, while the school labeled "4" enrolled students whose average test scores were well above the district average.

The horizontal distance between a given charter high school and the diagonal line represents that school's enrollment advantage or disadvantage—the degree to which students in that school had higher or lower scores on a given indicator than the feeder pool students. For example, the school labeled "4" has an enrollment advantage of 0.7 given that its enrollees have average test scores of 0.8 standard deviations above the district average and its feeder pool had average test scores of 0.1 standard deviations above the district average.

Our comparison of charter enrollees to feeder pool students is a comparison of two populations of students and, as such, any differences between the two groups are actual differences; there is no measurement error. We identify substantial differences between the two groups using two sets of dashed lines that run parallel to the diagonal line. The dashed line to the right of the diagonal identifies the point at which a school's enrollees are more than one-tenth of a standard deviation above the feeder pool on a given indicator, while the dashed line to the left of the diagonal identifies the point at which a school's enrollees are more than one-tenth of a standard deviation below the feeder pool on a given indicator. Thus, charter schools falling outside of the two dashed lines served students that were considerably different from their feeder pools.

FIGURE A

Sample Figure

Average Incoming Eighth-Grade Test Scores

Charter Students Incoming Test Scores
(Standard Deviation Units)

FIGURE 11

Most CPS Charter High Schools Enrolled Students with Similar or Lower Incoming Test Scores than Their Feeder Pools

Average Incoming (Eighth Grade) Test Scores

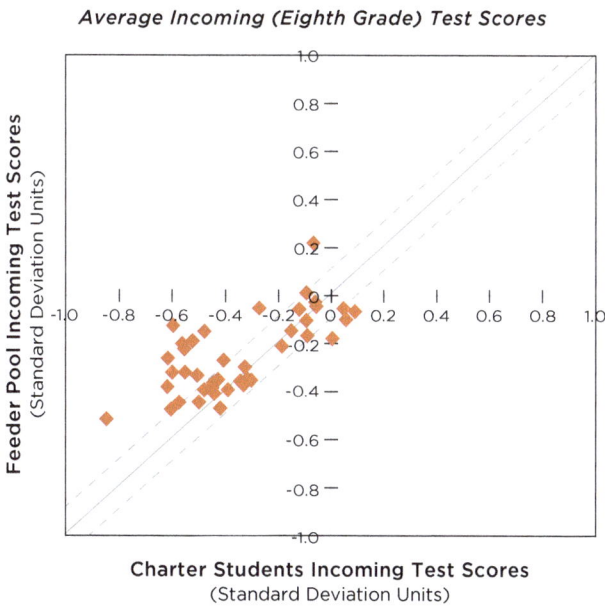

Charter Students Incoming Test Scores
(Standard Deviation Units)

Note: Incoming test scores of first-time ninth-grade students in 2013-14 were standardized across the cohort. A score of 0 represents the average incoming test score for this cohort. A score of -0.5 indicates a score at the 31st percentile while a score of 0.5 indicates a score at the 69th percentile.

FIGURE 12

Most CPS Charter High Schools Enrolled Students Whose Incoming Study Habits Were Typical of Their Feeder Pools

Average Incoming (Eighth Grade) Study Habits

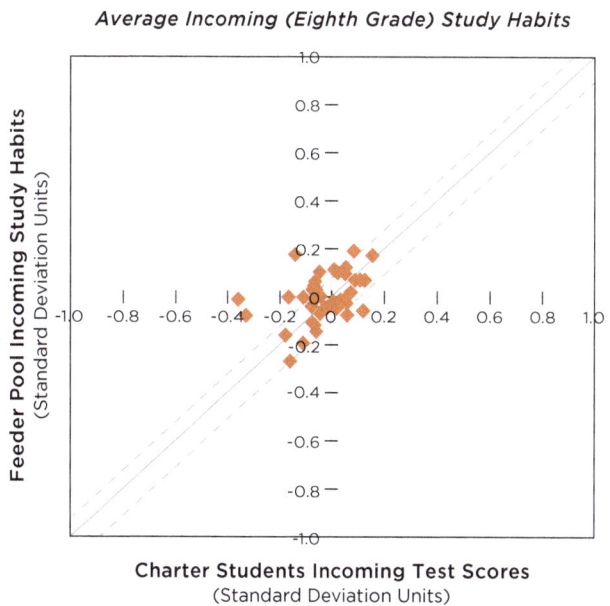

Charter Students Incoming Test Scores
(Standard Deviation Units)

Note: Incoming study habits of first-time ninth-graders in 2013-14 (see footnote 47 for a description of how this measure was created) were standardized so that a score of 0 represents the average incoming score for this cohort.

FIGURE 13

One-Third of CPS Charter High Schools Enrolled Students Whose Incoming GPAs Were Higher than Their Feeder Pools

Average Incoming (Eighth Grade) GPA

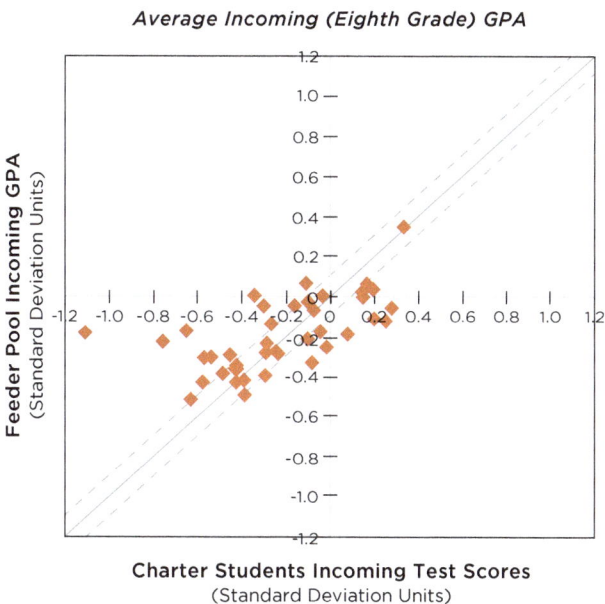

Charter Students Incoming Test Scores
(Standard Deviation Units)

Note: Incoming GPAs of first-time ninth-grade students in 2013-14 were standardized across the cohort. A score of 0 represents the average incoming grades for this cohort.

FIGURE 14

Most CPS Charter High Schools Enrolled Students with Higher Incoming Attendance Rates than Their Feeder Pools

Average Incoming (Eighth Grade) Attendance

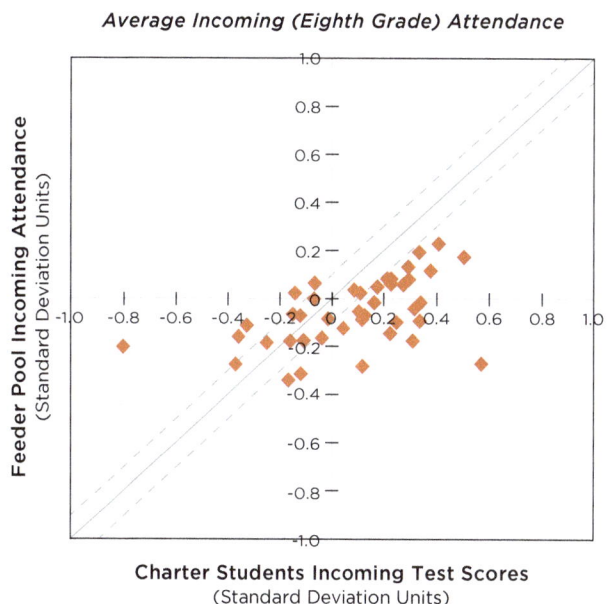

Charter Students Incoming Test Scores
(Standard Deviation Units)

Note: Incoming attendance rates of first-time ninth-grade students in 2013-14 were standardized across the cohort. A score of 0 represents the average attendance for this cohort.

Not only do **Figures 11–14** tell us how each charter school's students compared to its feeder pool; they also provide a sense of how charter school students compared to the overall cohort of all CPS students who were in ninth grade for the first time in 2013, as well as how much variation there was across charter schools. For example, focusing only on the horizontal axis in **Figure 11**, we find that charter schools served two very different groups of students, at least as defined by their eighth-grade test scores. One group of charter schools enrolled students whose average incoming test scores were fairly typical for the district; these schools fall between -0.1 and 0.1 on the horizontal axis. The second group of charter schools enrolled students whose scores, on average, were well below the district average; these schools had average test scores that were about one-half of a standard deviation or lower than the district average. **Figure 13** shows that charter schools enrolled students with a wide range of average GPAs; almost half had students with average incoming GPAs that were well below the district average (e.g., -0.20 standard deviations or lower), but some served students with GPAs that were typical for the district in eighth grade. By contrast, most charter schools enrolled students whose average eighth-grade attendance was either typical for the district or higher than the district average (**see Figure 14**).

Appendix B includes charts showing how charter enrollees compared to their feeder pools in terms of special education status, English Language Learner (ELL) status, and whether they qualified for free lunch. Most ninth-grade cohorts in charter high schools had similar proportions of students with disabilities, ELLs, and students qualifying for free lunch as their feeder populations. Only two schools had special education populations or ELL populations that were substantially lower (more than five percentage points) than their feeder pools, while seven charter schools had populations that were less likely to qualify for free lunch.

Overall, these findings suggest that charter schools did not enroll students with better academic skills, but they did enroll students with better academic behaviors,

such as eighth-grade attendance and, in some instances, eighth-grade GPA. The findings also show that there was a good deal of variation among charter schools in the kinds of students who enrolled in each school. For example, even though most charter schools enrolled students whose test scores were below the average of their feeder pools, some charter schools enrolled students whose test scores were far below their feeder pools, while other schools enrolled students who were only somewhat below their feeder pools. In the next section, we explore whether a school's enrollment advantage—the degree to which a school enrolled students with incoming skills that were stronger than their feeder pool—varied systematically depending on the characteristics of the charter high school.

Charter Schools' Enrollment Advantage is Related to Their Academic and Safety Records

Research on school choice has consistently shown that a desire to improve educational opportunities is one of the most prevalent reasons why students and their families pursue options other than their neighborhood school.[49] Schools with strong academic reputations are likely to be highly sought after by families who want an option other than their local school. But other factors can also play a role. Concerns about whether a school has a safe environment and whether it is conveniently located have also been shown to be important to families as they consider their options, particularly for low-income and minority parents.[50]

If some charter high schools are seen as more desirable, either because of their academic reputation, their safe environment, or their location, they may attract a sizeable applicant pool, including many students with strong academic credentials. Enrollment in about one-half of all CPS charter high schools is randomly determined through lotteries, but regardless of whether a school runs a lottery to determine admission, a strong applicant pool should result in a similarly strong group of admitted students.

---

49 Hamilton & Guin (2006); Smrekar & Goldrin (1999); Armor & Preiser (1998); Kleitz, Weiher, Tedin, & Matland (2000).

50 Lee et al. (1996).

We examined the relationship between charter high schools' enrollment advantage—the degree to which they enrolled students with substantially stronger incoming skills and behaviors than their feeder pools— and several of their characteristics, including prior academic performance, the level of safety of the school environment, and whether the school was centrally located in the city of Chicago. Each school's enrollment advantage on a given eighth-grade indicator was calculated by subtracting the average feeder-pool score from the average score of its enrollees. For example, charter schools that enrolled students with the same eighth-grade GPA as their feeder pool would have a score of 0 for its measure of enrollment advantage. Schools that enrolled students whose GPA was higher than the feeder pool would have a positive value and those who enrolled students whose GPA was lower than their feeder pool would have a negative value.[51] **The box titled "Measures of Charter School Characteristics"** describes how schools' prior performance, safety level, and location were measured. Results from the statistical models examining the relationship between charter school characteristics and their enrollment advantage scores are shown in **Table B.2 in Appendix B.**

Measures of Charter School Characteristics

We wondered whether characteristics of charter high schools, including their prior academic performance, the safety of their school environment, and whether they are centrally located within the city, were associated with each charter school's enrollment advantage on each of the five incoming skills and behaviors presented in Figures 11–14. Our measure of a school's enrollment advantage was calculated by subtracting the average feeder-pool score on a given eighth-grade indicator from the average score of the students who enrolled in that school.

A charter school's prior academic performance was measured by first combining two indicators into a single score for each high school in the district: the 2013 high school graduation rate (this is the graduation rate of students who were first-time ninth-graders in 2009) and also the spring 2013 ACT scores for students who were in eleventh grade that year. Each of these indicators was publicly available for nearly all high schools in the district (except for schools that had recently opened and had not yet had time to graduate a cohort of students or whose students had not yet reached the eleventh grade when the ACT was administered) and could conceivably have been used by students and their families to select the schools to which students would apply for ninth grade. Based on the combined score from these two indicators, all high schools in the district were then ranked into three equal-sized categories: highest-performing schools, average-performing schools, and lowest-performing schools. Schools that were missing this information were grouped into a "no performance information available" group. Only the rankings of charter schools were used for the analysis.

The level of safety at each school was measured using student responses to an annual 5Essentials survey administered by the UChicago Consortium and its partner UChicago Impact to all CPS students in grades 6–12. Students were asked to describe how safe they felt in the hallways and bathrooms of the school; outside around the school; traveling between home and school; and in their classes. Students' responses were combined into a measure using Rasch analysis, and the measures were aggregated to the school level. High schools were then ranked into three equal groups: safest high schools, average-safety high schools, and least-safe high schools. Schools that had no safety measure were grouped into a "no safety information available" group. Only the rankings of charter schools were used for the analysis.

Finally, we identified charter schools that were centrally located by first determining their longitude and latitude coordinates, using mapping software, and then using those coordinates to calculate the distance from a central location in downtown Chicago (the center of the "The Loop"). Schools that were located within three miles of this location were identified as being centrally located, while all other charter schools were identified as not being centrally located.

51 It's worth noting that charter schools' enrollment advantage scores look very different from one eighth-grade indicator to the next. For example, the average enrollment advantage for eighth-grade incoming test scores was -0.09 because, on average, charter schools enrolled students whose test scores are below their feeder pool's scores. By contrast, the average enrollment advantage for eighth-grade attendance was 0.13 because, on average, charter schools enrolled students whose eighth-grade attendance is higher than their feeder pools, on average.

Charter schools with the highest level of prior academic performance enrolled students with higher incoming test scores, GPA, and attendance relative to their feeder pool than schools with below average prior performance.[52] The advantages of a charter school's academic performance was limited to the group of schools with the highest performance. Schools with average prior performance were no different from schools with below-average performance in terms of who they attracted from their feeder pool, nor were schools with no available information about prior performance. (These were new schools, which did not yet have performance data available for prospective students at the time they were making decisions about high school.) There was no significant relationship between prior performance and a school's enrollment advantage in eighth-grade study habits.

The patterns for school safety were similar to prior academic performance: the safest schools attracted students with higher levels of eighth-grade test scores, GPA, attendance, and study habits, relative to their feeder pool, compared to the least safe schools. There was, of course, a good deal of overlap between a school's level of safety and its prior academic performance (these two indicators were correlated at 0.79), and it's likely that both a school's safety record and its academic performance contributed to its desirability in the eyes of students and their families as they considered their school choice options.

Finally, schools that were centrally located in Chicago had a marginally higher enrollment advantage than schools that were not centrally located in terms of students' test scores, GPAs, and attendance, but the differences were not significant.

Summary

The impression that charter schools enroll mostly higher-performing students persists, despite a number of studies in districts around the country showing otherwise. In Chicago, most charter schools enrolled students whose incoming test scores were average or below average, whether compared to the district or to the pool of students who might reasonably have enrolled in their charter school. This is not altogether surprising, given the number of high school options available to students with high test scores. But when we considered indicators beyond test scores, a different story emerged. Most charter schools enrolled students whose eighth-grade attendance rates were higher than their feeder pool, and some charter schools had students whose eighth-grade GPAs were also higher than their feeder pool. Collectively, the findings suggest charter schools may serve a distinct population within the district, attracting students who cannot enroll in top tier schools because they do not have the test scores to do so, but who have strong attendance records. Nevertheless, not all charters were equally desirable; those with the strongest academic reputations and the safest school environments were better positioned to attract more qualified candidates from their feeder pools than schools with less strong reputations and less safe environments.

In the next chapter, we examine another aspect of charter school enrollment: whether charter school students were more likely to transfer out of these schools at some point during their high school career. We also examine whether school transfers differed for students depending on the academic performance of their schools.

---

52 R-squared statistics from the models, which included schools' prior academic performance, are higher than R-squared statistics from the models, which included schools' safety levels for all enrollment advantage outcomes except study habits.

CHAPTER 4

High School Transfer Rates

National debates about charter schools have surfaced concerns that these schools could be more likely to counsel out low-achieving students in an attempt to improve their academic standing, giving them an advantage as they seek to attract new enrollments and also buffering them from district scrutiny in an era of high-stakes accountability.[53] Equally important, although less publicly acknowledged, is the impact that transferring from one school to another can have on students. High school is a period of preparation, during which many students are assembling academic and extracurricular portfolios for college applications. Research has shown that changing schools in the middle of high school can be disruptive to this process and can have implications for the types of colleges students are admitted to. For example, students who change schools during high school participate in

fewer extracurricular activities after their move and are less likely to take advanced classes post-move.[54] Other research has shown that students who transferred during high school were more likely to drop out than similar students who remained in the same school over the course of their high school career.[55]

Charter School Students' Transfer Rates

Contrary to what has been found in other districts, charter school students in CPS were more likely to change schools than non-charter school students.[56] As **Figure 15** shows, students who began high school in a charter school were twice as likely to transfer to another CPS school by the beginning of their second year than students who began in non-charter high schools. By the

FIGURE 15

CPS Charter School Students Were More Likely to Transfer to a Different High School than Students Enrolled in Non-Charter High Schools

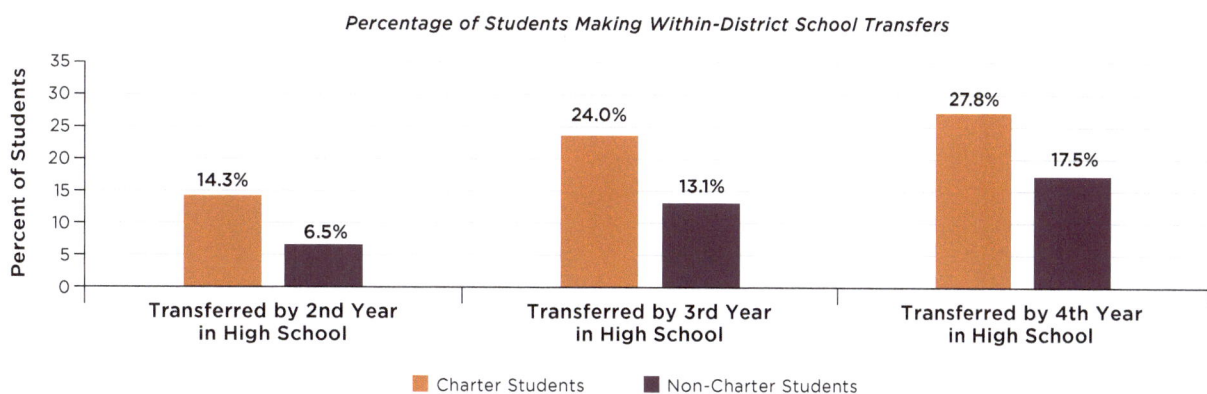

Percentage of Students Making Within-District School Transfers

	Charter Students	Non-Charter Students
Transferred by 2nd Year in High School	14.3%	6.5%
Transferred by 3rd Year in High School	24.0%	13.1%
Transferred by 4th Year in High School	27.8%	17.5%

Note: Average transfer rates are based on data from students who were first-time ninth-graders in 2010-13. Students who changed schools because their school was closed are not included in these transfer rates. Transfer rates are cumulative over time, so that the bars showing the percent of students transferring by their fourth year in high school also include students who transferred by their second and third years.

53 Brown (2013, January 5); Strauss (2012, February 2).
54 Sutton, Muller, & Langenkamp (2013).
55 Gasper, DeLuca, & Estacion (2012) used a propensity score model to match students who transferred schools during high school to students who remained in the same high school but who were similar on 177 different indicators prior to ninth grade.
56 We focused on within-district school transfers rather than out-of-district transfers because the latter can be influenced

by external factors such as residential moves, whereas within-district moves are more likely to occur because of student, family, or school decisions about the fit between a student and the school. CPS has released data showing that charter schools have higher expulsion rates than non-charter schools (Bentle & Marx, n.d.) However, compared to school transfer rates, expulsion rates are relatively low and cannot account for all of the transfers that students make.

beginning of their fourth year in high school, more than one-quarter of students who began high school in a charter school transferred elsewhere in the district, compared to only 18 percent of non-charter school students.

As Chapter 2 showed, charter school students looked different from students who attended other high schools in CPS in terms of the skills and behaviors they entered high schools with; charter students had lower eighth-grade test scores, on average, but higher eighth-grade attendance than other students. It's possible that these differences were related to school transfers—for example, research has shown that students with lower test scores are more likely to change schools.[57] As a result, comparing charter school students to all other students in the district gives a biased estimate of whether charter school students were more likely to change schools. Instead, we wanted to compare them to students with similar background characteristics and similar incoming skills, behavior, and previous school experiences. One particularly important characteristic that we took into account was whether students transferred schools between seventh and eighth grade, which could influence whether they changed schools during high school.

Figure 16 compares transfer rates for charter high school students and students in non-charter high schools, after controlling for differences in incoming skills, school experiences, and background characteristics. It shows that charter school students were between 6–9 percentage points more likely to change schools at some point during high school than students who enrolled in non-charter high schools, even after taking into account these differences.

The literature on charter schools offers several different possibilities for why charter school students might transfer out of their schools at higher rates than other students. The first scenario, mentioned above, suggests that charter schools may be more likely to encourage low-achieving students to transfer elsewhere as a means of protecting the school's academic reputation.[58] A second theory proposes that even if charter schools do not actively counsel students out, students with poor academic performance or behavior issues may ultimately feel that a charter school is not a good fit academically, given that these schools often have stringent requirements about behavior and performance.[59] Either way, these two theories suggest that transfer

On Average, CPS Charter High School Students Were Significantly More Likely to Change Schools than Similar Students Enrolled in Non-Charter High Schools

Within-District School Transfer Rates of Charter School Students Compared to Similar Students in Non-Charter Schools

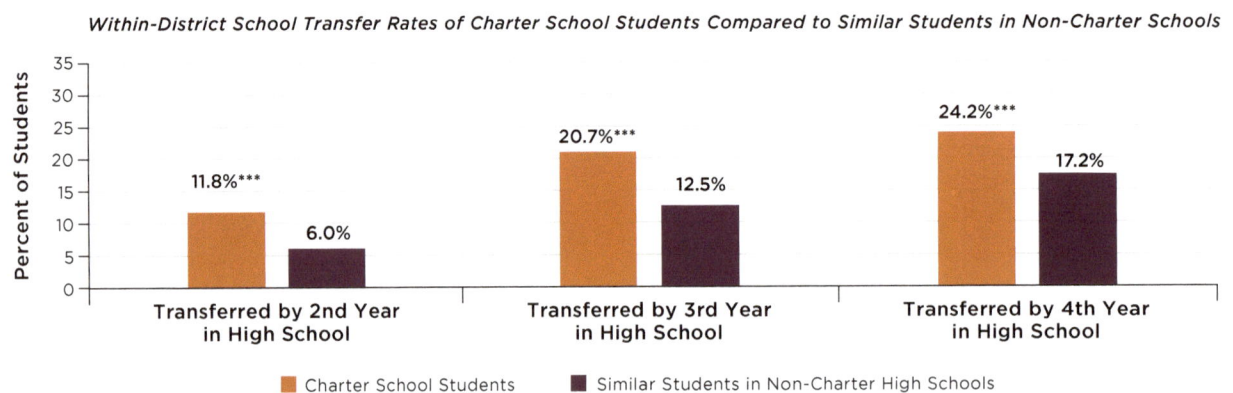

Note: Analyses of transfer rates included students who were first-time ninth-graders in 2010–13 and were conducted using a 2-level HLM model in which students were nested in their ninth-grade schools. Models controlled for an array of eighth-grade academic performance indicators, eighth-grade school experiences, and background characteristics. Control variables were grand-mean centered so that the intercept represents students with typical eighth-grade academic performance, school experiences, and background characteristics who enrolled in a non-charter high school. A *** indicates that charter school students had significantly different transfer rates than similar students in non-charter schools at p<0.001.

57 Winters (2015).

58 See, for example, Brown (2013, January 5) and Strauss (2012, February 2). A related concern is that charter schools with strict disciplinary practices, such as "no excuses" schools, may be more likely to counsel out students with disciplinary infractions. A recent study by Mathematica Policy Institute examined attrition in KIPP schools, one of the most prominent examples of charter schools with a "no excuses" approach. It showed no differences in transfer rates for KIPP students and students in nearby district schools (Nichols-Barrer, Gil, Gleason, & Tuttle, 2012).

59 Zimmer & Guarino (2013).

rates are higher for lower-achieving students in charter high schools than for lower-achieving students in non-charter high schools. This may be particularly true when the overall academic performance of a school is high.

A third theory, which is less widely acknowledged, argues that since charter school students and their families are active participants in the school choice process, they may be especially sensitive to the academic quality of the schools that students attend.[60] Students who enroll in charter schools where the overall level of student achievement is low may be more likely to transfer out, particularly if their own level of academic performance is relatively strong.

Figure 17 presents evidence to examine these hypotheses. It shows transfer rates based on students' ninth-grade test scores and their schools' prior academic performance.[61] Although the findings are only suggestive, there is some support for all three theories. For example, consistent with the first and second theories described above, charter school students with below-average test scores were more likely to transfer out of high-performing schools than non-charter students with below-average test scores (11 percent

compared to 6 percent). But, perhaps surprisingly, charter school students with above-average test scores were also more likely to transfer out of these schools than non-charter students with comparable test scores (8 percent compared to 3 percent). Although charter school students with below-average test scores had higher transfer rates than charter students with above-average test scores (11 percent compared to 8 percent), the differences between these groups were comparable to the differences between non-charter students with below- and above-average test scores. Unfortunately, the evidence cannot definitively show whether higher rates of transfers among low-performing charter students were due to their being pushed out or choosing to leave on their own. While there may be instances of schools counseling low-performing students to consider other options, this does not seem to be a widespread phenomenon.

Figure 17 also provides evidence in support of the third hypothesis, which suggests charter school students may be particularly sensitive to the academic quality of the schools they attend. Charter school students were most likely to change schools when they

FIGURE 17

School Transfer Rates Were Highest for CPS Charter School Students Who Enrolled in Low-Performing or Recently Opened Schools in Ninth Grade

School Transfer Rates by Students' Ninth-Grade Test Scores, Their Schools' Academic Performance, and Charter Status

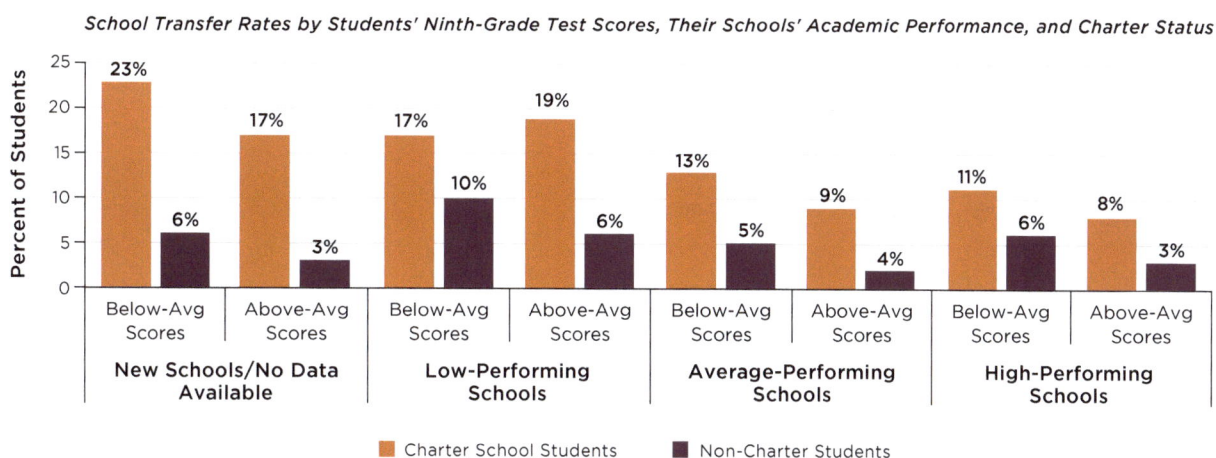

Note: This figure uses average transfer rates for students who were first-time ninth-grade students in 2013, based on their ninth-grade EXPLORE scores and their schools' prior academic performance. The analysis was limited to only this cohort because few charter school students took the ninth-grade EXPLORE test prior to 2013. Students were grouped into one of two categories: those who scored at or above the district average and those who scored below. Schools were categorized based on prior graduation rates and ACT scores. Overall, two-thirds of all charter school transfers were made by students with below average test scores.

60 Hanushek, Kain, Rivkin, & Branch (2007).
61 Schools' academic performance was measured in the same way as in Chapter 3: by combining each school's 2013 high school graduation rate and their 2013 ACT scores.

enrolled in a low-performing school. Moreover, charter school students with above-average test scores in low-performing schools actually transferred at higher rates than charter students with below-average test scores (19 percent compared to 17 percent). (Non-charter school students enrolled in low-performing schools also had higher transfer rates than non-charter students enrolled in average- or high-performing schools.)

Transfer rates were also quite high for charter students who began high school in a new charter school. Research has shown that many new charter schools have weaker academic performance than more established charter schools, but given the newness of these schools, key performance indicators (e.g., high school graduation rates, ACT scores) were not publicly available at the time that students were selecting high schools. As a result, students and families may have chosen these schools without much information about what these schools were actually like.[62]

Figure 18 shows the types of schools that charter students transferred into by the beginning of their second year in high school. Around 80 percent of transferring charter students, regardless of their achievement level, transferred to non-charter schools, and around one-half of all transferring charter students transferred to a neighborhood school. The fact that neighborhood schools received such a high proportion of transfer students may create a distinct challenge for them, particularly if they are responsible for helping students get on-track in terms of fulfilling the credits they need for graduation. Students with above-average test scores were more likely to enroll in selective schools (these include selective enrollment, military, and magnet schools) than students with below-average test scores, a finding that is consistent with the third hypothesis—that at least some above-average students left charter schools in search of better educational opportunities. Charter students with below-average test scores were more likely to enroll in alternative schools or special education schools.

FIGURE 18

Eighty Percent of CPS Charter High School Students Who Changed Schools by the Beginning of Their Second Year in High School Transferred to a CPS Non-Charter High School

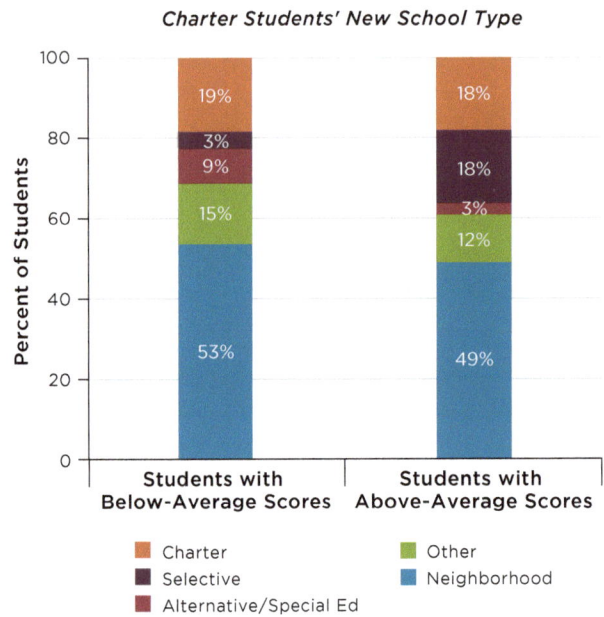

Charter Students' New School Type

Summary

Charter school students in CPS were significantly more likely to change schools than similar students in non-charter schools. More research is needed to understand the specific reasons why so many charter school students changed schools at some point during their high school career. But regardless of their reasons for transferring, most charter transfers left the charter sector all together, with many students opting to enroll in neighborhood schools. This could create challenges for these receiving schools, who are responsible for ensuring their transfer students are on-track to graduate.

In the next chapter, we examine charter school students' performance in high school on a range of outcomes, including academic behaviors, mindsets, course performance, test scores, and educational attainment, and we compare their performance to similar students in non-charter schools. The findings from this chapter

---

62 Very few charter students with above-average test scores enrolled in a low-performing or new charter school. In fact, more than one-half of all charter students with above-average test scores enrolled in high-performing schools, so even

though their transfer rates out of high-performing schools are relatively low, they account for the largest share of transfers made by charter students with above-average test scores.

—higher rates of school transfers for charter school students—have implications for how we assess charter school students' academic performance and attainment during high school and beyond. Given that lower-achieving charter students were more likely to leave their charter high schools, this could bias analyses of student outcomes in grades 10–12 in favor of charter schools. To address this, students were considered to be enrolled in their ninth-grade school for all analyses in Chapter 5, even if they had moved to a different school at the point when a given outcome was measured. In other words, a student was considered enrolled in a charter school if that was where they started their high school career, even if they moved elsewhere at some point.

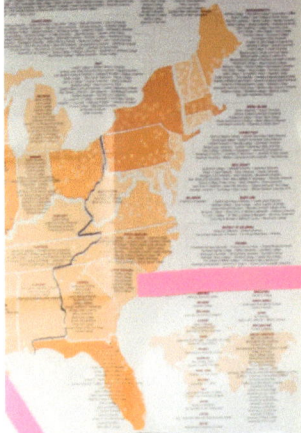

COLLEGES AND UNIVERSITIES.
OR YOU. **commonapp.org**

IOWA STATE

ST. CATHERINE
UNIVERSITY

A1
FIRE

ENGINEERING
ILLINOIS

R RUTGERS

Ask Me!

I Graduated from...

WESLEYAN

&

ILLINOIS

MS. BERIEN

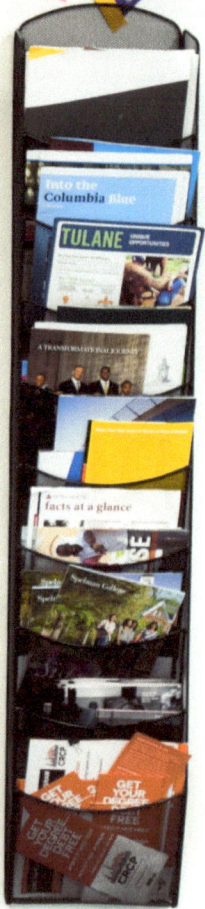

CHAPTER 5

High School Performance and Educational Attainment

Much of the research examining whether students enrolled in charter schools have better educational outcomes than students enrolled in non-charter schools has focused solely on students' test scores. Although this is understandable, given the priority that state and national education policies place on test scores as a measure of school performance, research increasingly shows that students need a range of noncognitive skills, behaviors, and mindsets, in addition to academic skills and knowledge, to successfully navigate pathways through high school, college, and into the workplace. However, the notion that schools need to pay attention to and be held accountable for student performance on outcomes other than test scores is only just beginning to take hold.[63] This chapter contributes to the research base on charter schools by providing an in-depth look at how these schools and their students performed on a number of outcomes, including academic behaviors, mindsets, course performance, test scores, and educational attainment.

The next sections describe student performance on a range of high school and post-secondary outcomes. Just as in Chapter 4, we compared charter school students' performance to students enrolled in non-charter high schools, controlling for their incoming skills, school experiences, and background characteristics. For all analyses, students were considered enrolled in their ninth-grade school, even if they transferred elsewhere over the course of high school.[64] This was designed to address the fact that charter school students had higher rates of school transfers and these students were more likely to have lower levels of student achievement. As a result, our estimates of charter school differences on student outcomes are likely to be somewhat conservative.

Academic Behaviors and Mindsets

Attendance, study habits, and classroom engagement are all important behaviors that have been linked to students' subsequent academic performance. Students who come to class regularly, are engaged and participate in classroom discussions, and complete their homework assignments on time are all more likely to pass their classes and earn high grades than students who do not engage in these behaviors. Not only do these skills matter, but they appear to be malleable and can be shaped by educational practice.[65] Perseverance, often referred to as "grit," is also a critical factor in how well students perform academically—students who are able to persist in a task even in the face of challenges have been shown to have higher levels of educational attainment—but the research around whether schools are able to influence the development of grit is somewhat unclear.[66]

Figure 19 shows how charter high school students compared to students in non-charter high schools on attendance in ninth and eleventh grades, controlling for incoming skills, school experiences, and background characteristics. On average, charter school students had significantly higher attendance in both grades than similar students in non-charter schools. For example, among CPS students who entered high school with typical skills, school experiences, and background characteristics, the ninth-grade attendance rate was 92.9 percent for students who enrolled in charter high schools, compared to 88.5 percent for similar students enrolled elsewhere, a difference of almost 5 percentage points. In a typical school year with 180 days, this means that charter school students came to school about a week and a half (or eight days) more than similar students in non-charter schools.

---

63 The passage of the Every Student Succeeds Act in 2015 has been instrumental in laying the groundwork for this (Editorial Projects in Education Research Center, 2016, March 31).

64 This decision rule is consistent with other Consortium research that looks at high school graduation and post-secondary attainment.

65 Allensworth & Easton (2007); Farrington, Roderick, Allensworth, Nagaoka, Keyes, Johnson, & Beechum (2012); Reyes, Bracket, Rivers, White, & Salovey (2012).

66 Farrington et al. (2012).

FIGURE 19

On Average, CPS Charter High School Students Had Higher Rates of Ninth- and Eleventh-Grade Attendance than Similar Students in Non-Charter High Schools

Ninth-Grade and Eleventh-Grade Attendance Rates

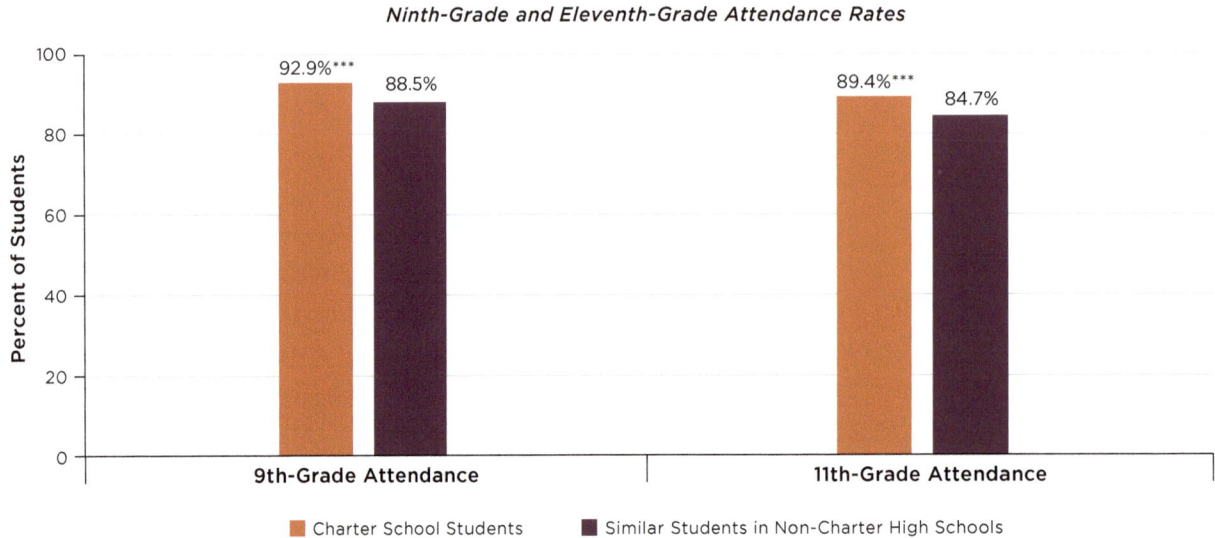

Note: Analyses of ninth- and eleventh-grade attendance rates included students who were first-time ninth-graders in 2010–13 and were conducted using a 2-level HLM model in which students were nested in their ninth-grade schools. Models controlled for an array of eighth-grade academic performance indicators, eighth-grade school experiences, and background characteristics. Control variables were grand-mean centered so that the intercept represents students with typical eighth-grade academic performance, school experiences, and background characteristics who enrolled in a non-charter high school. *** indicates that charter school students had significantly different attendance rates than similar students in non-charter schools at p<0.001.

Similar differences existed for eleventh-grade attendance (89.4 percent vs. 84.7 percent), although overall attendance rates were lower for both groups of students.

Measuring academic behaviors and mindsets—such as study habits, engagement, and grit—can be difficult. The UChicago Consortium relies on students' self-reports on annual surveys that ask a range of questions about experiences and activities related to school. The specific questions that were used in these three measures are included in the note under **Figure 20**. As **Figure 20** shows, charter school students had comparable study habits and grit to students in non-charter high schools, controlling for differences in incoming skills, school experiences, and background characteristics. Charter school students had significantly higher levels of classroom engagement than similar students in other schools.

Test Scores

Figure 21 shows average high school test scores for charter and non-charter school students, after controlling for incoming skills, school experiences, and background characteristics. The PLAN is part of the ACT-aligned EPAS system of tests. CPS students took the PLAN in tenth grade and the ACT in eleventh grade. Scores on both tests were standardized so that 0 represented the district average. Among students who entered high school with typical skills, school experiences, and background characteristics, those who enrolled in a charter high school scored just above the district average of 0, while students who enrolled in a non-charter high school scored more than one-tenth of a standard deviation below the district average. The overall difference between the two groups was 0.18 standard deviations, equivalent to about 0.6 point on the PLAN. On the ACT, the typical CPS student in a charter high school scored about one-quarter of a standard deviation higher, equivalent to one point higher, than similar students in non-charter high schools (**see Figure 21**).

FIGURE 20

On Average, CPS Charter High School Students Had Comparable Study Habits and Grit as Similar Students in Non-Charter High Schools

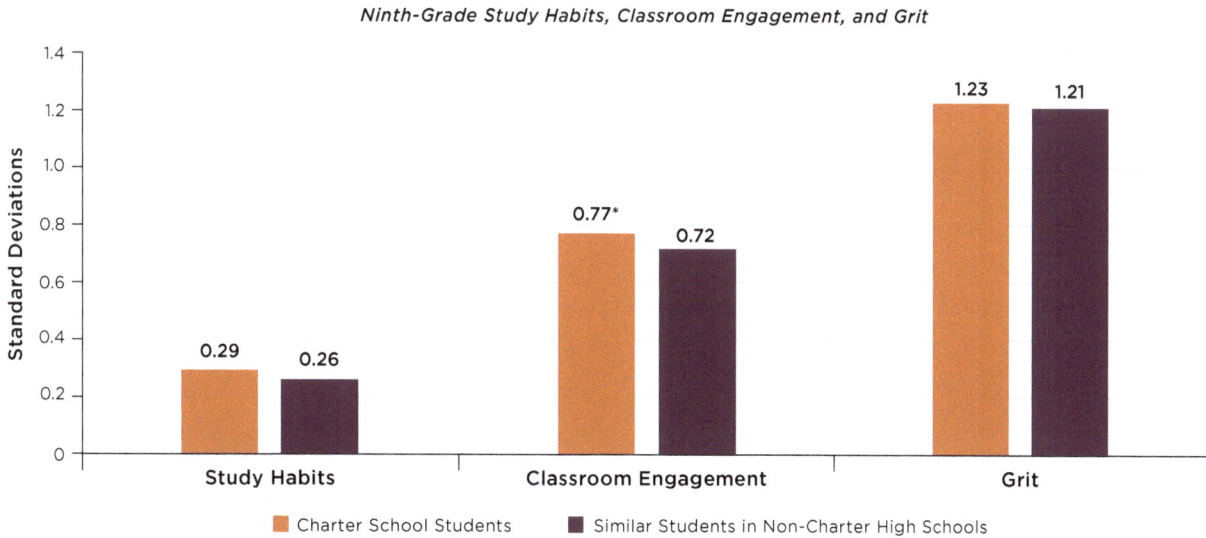

Ninth-Grade Study Habits, Classroom Engagement, and Grit

Note: Measures of study habits, classroom engagement, and grit were created using Rasch analysis of student responses on survey items. Study habits included responses on four items: I always study for tests; I set aside time to do my homework and study; I try to do well on my schoolwork even when it isn't interesting to me; If I need to study, I don't go out with my friends. Classroom engagement was measured with the following four items: I usually look forward to this class; I work hard to do my best in this class; Sometimes I get so interested in my work I don't want to stop; The topics we are studying are interesting and challenging. Grit was measured with the following four items: I finish whatever I begin; I am a hard worker; I continue steadily towards my goals; I don't give up easily. Analyses included students who were first-time ninth-graders in 2010–13 and were conducted using a 2-level HLM model in which students were nested in their ninth-grade schools. Measures were standardized so that 0 represented the average for the sample. Models controlled for an array of eighth-grade academic performance indicators, eighth-grade school experiences, and background characteristics. Control variables were grand-mean centered so that the intercept represents students with typical eighth-grade academic performance, school experiences, and background characteristics who enrolled in a non-charter high school. * indicates that charter school students had significantly different scores on these measures than similar students in non-charter schools at p<0.05.

FIGURE 21

On Average, CPS Charter High School Students Scored Significantly Higher on Standardized Tests in Tenth and Eleventh Grade than Similar Students in Non-Charter High Schools

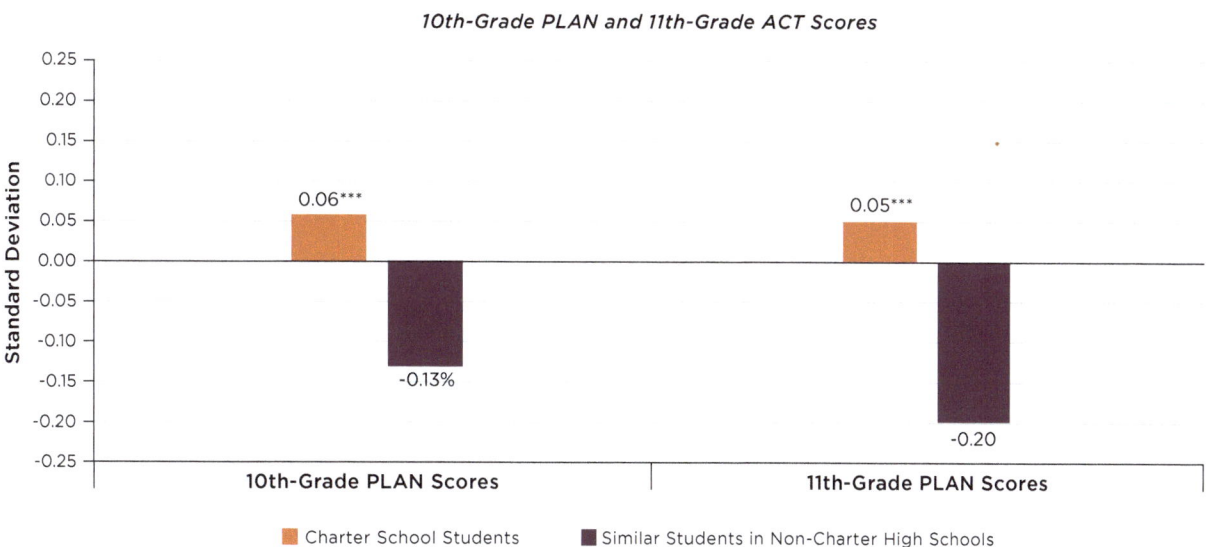

10th-Grade PLAN and 11th-Grade ACT Scores

Note: Analyses of high school test scores included students who were first-time ninth-graders in 2010–13 and were conducted using a 2-level HLM model in which students were nested in their ninth-grade schools. Test scores were standardized within cohorts so that 0 represented the average for that cohort. Models controlled for an array of eighth-grade academic performance indicators, eighth-grade school experiences, and background characteristics. Control variables were grand-mean centered so that the intercept represents students with typical eighth-grade academic performance, school experiences, and background characteristics who enrolled in a non-charter high school. *** indicates that charter school students had significantly different test scores than similar students in non-charter schools at p<0.001.

Course Performance

Previous research at the UChicago Consortium has shown that students' ninth-grade course performance is an important indicator of how likely they are to graduate from high school. Students who fail no more than one core course in ninth grade and accumulate five full-year course credits are four times more likely to graduate than students who fail two or more classes or accumulate fewer than five full-year course credits.[67] Unfortunately, we were not able to analyze charter school students' transcript information, including grades or credits earned.[68] To address this shortcoming, we constructed a proxy for whether students passed their ninth-grade classes by examining whether students were promoted to tenth grade by the fall after their first year in ninth grade. Students who experienced an on-time promotion were likely to have passed the required number of courses in ninth grade. Prior Consortium research has shown that this proxy for ninth-grade course performance is a valid indicator for both charter and non-charter school students.[69]

On-time promotion rates were quite high regardless of sector. However, charter high school students were significantly less likely to be promoted to tenth grade by the end of their first year in high school than students in non-charter high schools, controlling for differences in incoming skills, school experiences, and background characteristics: 96.1 percent, compared to 98.0 percent (see Figure 22).[70] This pattern is not altogether surprising, given that that promotion requirements were higher in most charter schools.

The next section examines high school graduation rates and post-secondary outcomes of charter school students. Most of the cohorts used to analyze high school outcomes described above had not had sufficient time to graduate from high school and transition into post-secondary opportunities at the time this study was conducted. To address this, we used an earlier set of cohorts, students who were first-time ninth-graders in 2008, 2009, or 2010, to analyze high school graduation and post-secondary outcomes. There is a good deal of overlap between

FIGURE 22

On Average, CPS Charter High School Students Were Somewhat Less Likely to Be Promoted to Tenth Grade One Year After Entering High School than Similar Students in Non-Charter High Schools

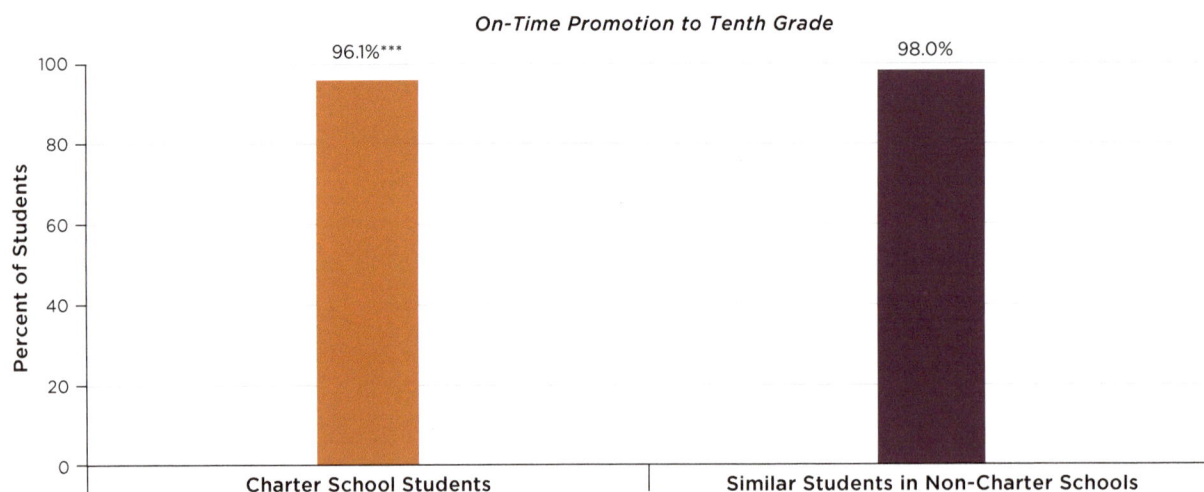

On-Time Promotion to Tenth Grade

Note: Analyses of promotion to tenth grade included students who were first-time ninth-graders in 2010–13 and were conducted using a 2-level HLM model in which students were nested in their ninth-grade schools. Models controlled for an array of eighth-grade academic performance indicators, eighth-grade school experiences, and background characteristics. Control variables were grand-mean centered so that the intercept represents students with typical eighth-grade academic performance, school experiences, and background characteristics who enrolled in a non-charter high school. *** indicates that charter school students had significantly different promotion rates than similar students in non-charter schools at p<0.001.

67 Allensworth & Easton (2007).
68 Many CPS charter schools use different student information systems from the IMPACT system used by non-charter schools. Because each system varies in the way that it stores information about courses, credits, teachers, periods, grades, and other data, creating linkages across systems is difficult,

and our data archive currently does not include records of charter school students' course performance.
69 Allensworth, Healey, Gwynne, & Crespin (2016).
70 A difference of 1.9 percent in promotion rates is equivalent to 425 fewer charter students promoted to tenth grade by their second year in high school.

the two groups. Thirty-six of the 47 charter high schools that enrolled ninth-grade students from 2008–13 are included in both samples, and students who were first-time ninth-graders in 2010 are also in both analytic samples.

Educational Attainment

Graduating from high school and enrolling in college are critical steps along the path to full-time employment and earning a living wage. Over the last decade and a half, CPS high schools have made considerable gains in the proportion of, and the total number of, students who graduate from high school. Previous research conducted by the UChicago Consortium showed that graduation rates rose by 16 points over a 10-year period, from 59 percent in 2005 to 75 percent in 2014. Most of this improvement occurred among non-charter, non-selective schools. For example, graduation rates for students in these schools increased from 55 percent to 72 percent, while the graduation rate of charter school students increased from 66 percent in 2005 to 74 percent during this time period.[71]

In this study, we found that among students who were first-time ninth-graders in 2008–10, those enrolled in charter schools in ninth grade graduated from high school within four years at comparable rates, on average, to similar students enrolled in non-charter schools (see Figure 23). As described in Chapter 2, many charter schools had more graduation requirements than non-charter schools, but this did not seem to have a negative impact on graduation rates.

CPS as a whole has also made strides in college enrollments. Prior Consortium research has shown that among students who graduated from high school in 2014, 42 percent enrolled in a four-year college or university, up from 33 percent in 2006. Improvements in CPS college enrollment rates have largely been driven by charter school students and students in selective enrollment high schools.[72] Although the overall increases in college enrollment rates have not been as

large as high school graduation rates, high schools now send many more students to college than ever before.

Findings from this study show that charter school students enrolled in four-year colleges or universities at substantially higher rates than similar students in non-charter high schools. Among students who entered high school with typical skills, school experiences, and background characteristics and who also graduated from high school, the enrollment rate in a four-year college or university was 45.1 percent for students who attended charter high schools, compared to only 26.2 percent for students who attended non-charter schools (see Figure 23). Higher rates of college enrollment by charter school students may have been due to their higher ACT scores; but even after taking test scores into account, we found that charter school students were still more likely to enroll in four-year colleges than similar students in non-charter schools (not shown). Charter school students were also more likely to enroll in a very selective college or university than similar students who attended a non-charter high schools: 7.2 percent compared to 2.2 percent (see Figure 23).[73]

Unfortunately, college graduation rates for students who started high school in 2008–10 were not yet available at the time this study was conducted. Instead, we examined college persistence rates, which we define as completing four semesters of college, and which have been shown to be predictive of who ultimately graduates. We analyzed college persistence in two ways. The first analysis included all high school graduates and compared students who maintained four semesters of continuous college enrollment to students with any other outcomes, including fewer than four semesters of enrollment and not enrolling at all. As shown in Figure 23, charter high school graduates were more likely to be continuously enrolled in college for four semesters than non-charter high school graduates (21.4 percent compared to 13.0 percent), after taking into account differences in eighth-grade skills, school experiences, and background characteristics.

---

71 Graduation rates come from research conducted by Allensworth, et al. (2016). Their study grouped students by age cohorts—in this case, cohorts of 19-year-old students—so as to minimize the impact that certain policies (e.g., the grade retention) had on students at particular points in time. They also used a different method for calculating graduation than the method used by CPS, which accounts for differences in the reported graduation rates.

72 Nagaoka & Healey (2016).

73 Barron's ranks four-year colleges and universities based on their selectivity. Categories include: 1) Non-Competitive, 2) Less Competitive, 3) Competitive, 4) Very Competitive, 5) Highly Competitive, and 6) Most Competitive. This analysis examined enrollment in schools that are ranked Very Competitive or higher.

FIGURE 23

On Average, CPS Charter High School Students Had Higher Rates of College Enrollment than Similar Students in Non-Charter High Schools

Educational Attainment

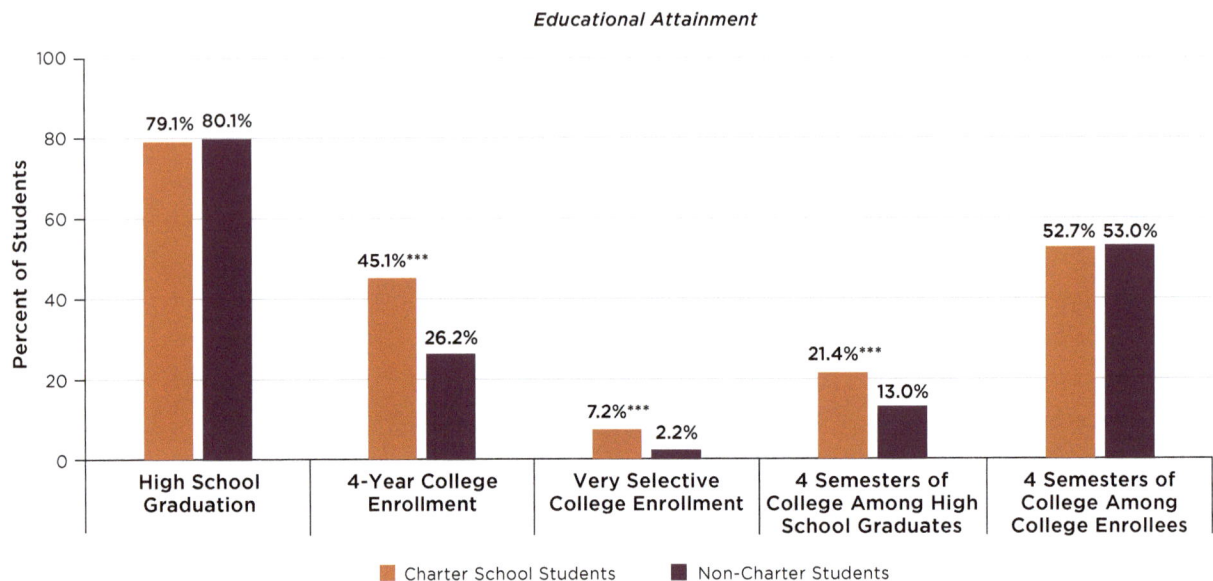

Note: Analyses of educational attainment were based on students who were first-time ninth-graders in 2008–10. The analysis of high school graduation included all students from these three cohorts. Analyses of four-year college enrollment, enrollment in a very selective college, completion of four semesters of college among high school graduates, included students from these same three-grade cohorts who graduated from high school. The analysis of four semesters of college among college enrollees only included students from these cohorts who enrolled in college. Analyses were conducted using a 2-level HLM in which students were nested in their ninth-grade schools. Models controlled for an array of eighth-grade academic performance indicators, eighth-grade school experiences, and background characteristics. Control variables were grand-mean centered so that the intercept represented students with typical eighth-grade academic performance, school experiences, and background characteristics who enrolled in a non-charter high school. *** indicates that charter school students had significantly different attainment than similar students in non-charter schools at p<0.001.

The second analysis was similar, but only included students who enrolled in college. The analysis compared students who maintained four semesters of continuous college enrollment to students who were enrolled for only one, two, or three semesters. As shown in **Figure 23**, among college enrollees, the proportion of charter students who remained stably enrolled in college for four semesters was nearly the same—around 53 percent—as students who attended non-charter high schools.

Variation in Student Outcomes Among Charter Schools

Research on charter schools has typically focused on overall differences between charter and non-charter schools and has rarely addressed variation within the charter community. As a result, there is a tendency to think about all charter schools as performing at roughly comparable levels, but this may not actually be the case. This section explores the question of variation in student performance among charter schools, and we

focus on those outcomes where charter school students' performance differed most substantially from similar students in non-charter schools, including high school attendance, test scores, college enrollment, and college selectivity. We relied on school-level estimates generated from the same statistical models used earlier in this chapter to describe overall sector differences. As a reminder, these models took into account an extensive set of indicators capturing students' skills, school experiences, and background characteristics prior to entering ninth grade. As a result, school level estimates that were adjusted for these differences can be understood as the average performance level if all schools were serving the same set of students.

Figure 24 and **Figure 25** show the distribution of average ninth- and eleventh-grade attendance for charter and non-charter schools, serving students with typical eighth-grade characteristics. Average attendance rates of students who entered high school with typical skills and background characteristics were fairly similar among charter high schools, with most

We use density plots to describe the variation among schools for a given outcome. Density plots are somewhat similar to histograms in that they show the percent of schools at each performance level on a given outcome, but they use kernel smoothing to plot values, which creates a smoother distribution line. The horizontal axis describes the average performance level on a given outcome, and the vertical axis describes the percent of schools with that level of performance. The peak in the distribution line represents the performance level at which the most number of schools fall. As the distribution line approaches 0, there are fewer and fewer schools whose average performance is at the level. In each figure below, the orange line shows the distribution of charter schools at each performance level for a given outcome. The distribution of non-charter schools on the same outcome is shown as a purple line for the sake of comparison. Plots also include vertical dashed lines showing the overall sector average for charter and non-charter schools.

FIGURE 24

CPS Charter High Schools Had Less Variation in Average, Adjusted Ninth-Grade Attendance Rates than Non-Charter High Schools

Distribution of Schools' Average Adjusted 9th-Grade Attendance Rates

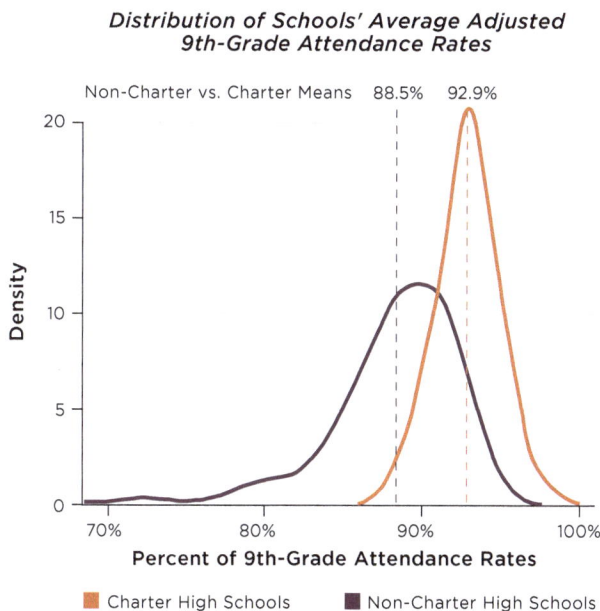

Note: Density plots are based on school-level residuals from the same 2-level HLM model used to examine overall differences in attendance rates between charter school and non-charter school students (see Figure 19). These analyses were based on students who were first-time ninth-graders in 2010–13 and controlled for an array of eighth-grade academic performance indicators, eighth-grade school experiences, and background characteristics. Control variables were grand-mean centered so that each school's residual value was the average score for students with typical eighth-grade academic performance, school experiences, and background characteristics.

FIGURE 25

CPS Charter High Schools Had Somewhat Less Variation in Average, Adjusted Eleventh-Grade Attendance Rates than Non-Charter High Schools

Distribution of Schools' Average Adjusted 11th-Grade Attendance Rates

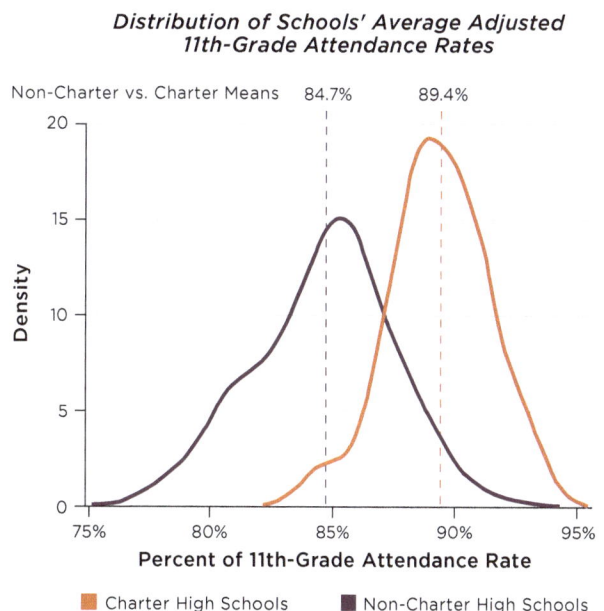

Note: Density plots show school-level residuals from the same 2-level HLM model used to examine overall differences in test scores between charter school and non-charter school students (see Figure 21). These analyses were based on students who were first-time ninth-graders in 2010–13 and controlled for an array of eighth-grade academic performance indicators, eighth-grade school experiences, and background characteristics. Control variables were grand-mean centered so that each school's residual value was the average score for students with typical eighth-grade academic performance, school experiences, and background characteristics.

schools falling within a few percentage points on either side of the overall charter average in each grade level (92.9 percent for ninth-grade attendance and 89.4 percent for eleventh-grade attendance). By contrast, there was much more variation among non-charter schools, particularly for average ninth-grade attendance, and

especially at the low end of the distribution. Despite greater variation, the non-charter schools with the highest attendance rates weren't as high as the charter schools with the highest rates, while non-charter schools with the lowest rates were well below those charter schools with the lowest rates.

In contrast to attendance, the distribution of test scores for charter schools shows much greater variability compared to the distribution for non-charter schools (**see Figure 26 and Figure 27**). Moreover, the highest-performing charter schools had much higher average scores than the highest-performing non-charter schools. (It is important to keep in mind that these scores were adjusted to take into account differences in the students that schools served. Without these adjustments, the highest-performing non-charter schools—selective enrollment schools—had higher test scores than the highest-performing charter schools.) There were a small number of charter schools that had average test scores on the PLAN and ACT that exceeded 0.40 standard deviations, whereas the highest-performing non-charter high school had average scores on each test that were around 0.30 standard deviations. At the other end of the distribution, the lowest-performing charter high school had lower average scores than the lowest-performing non-charter high school.

Distributions of schools' average college enrollment rates show a similar pattern as test scores, with much more variation among charter schools than among non-charter schools (**see Figure 28**). There were a small number of charter schools whose four-year college enrollment rates for typical CPS students were more than 60 percent, well above the charter average of 45 percent, and also above the highest-performing non-charter school serving similar students.

There was also much more variation among charter schools than non-charter schools in the percent of students who enrolled in very selective colleges (**see Figure 29**). Enrollment rates in selective colleges for CPS students who attended a non-charter high school ranged between 0 and 7 percent, controlling for differences in eighth-grade skills, school experiences, and background characteristics For charter high schools, enrollment rates ranged between 0 percent and 30 percent, although there were few charter schools that had more than 20 percent of their students enrolled in very selective institutions.

FIGURE 26

CPS Charter High Schools Had Greater Variation in Average, Adjusted PLAN Scores than Non-Charter High Schools

Distribution of Schools' Average Adjusted 10th-Grade PLAN Scores

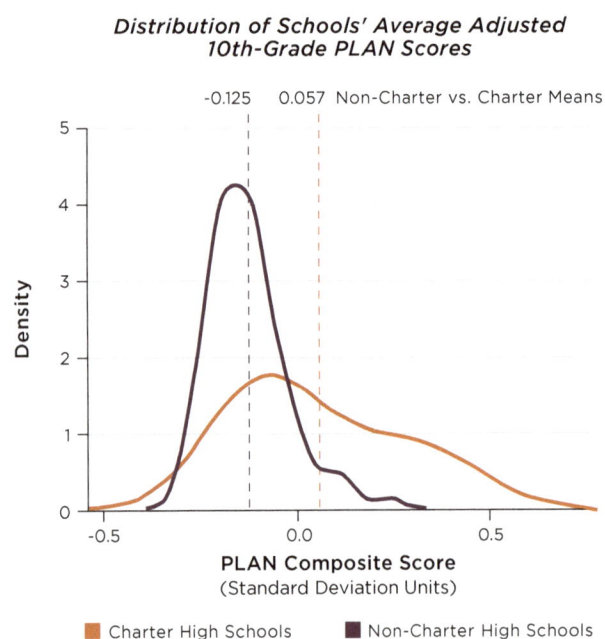

Note: Density plots show school-level residuals from the same 2-level HLM model used to examine overall differences in test scores between charter school and non-charter school students (see Figure 21). These analyses were based on students who were first-time ninth-graders in 2010–13 and controlled for an array of eighth-grade academic performance indicators, eighth-grade school experiences, and background characteristics. Control variables were grand-mean centered so that each school's residual value was the average score for students with typical eighth-grade academic performance, school experiences, and background characteristics.

FIGURE 27

CPS Charter High Schools Had More Variation in Average, Adjusted ACT Scores than Non-Charter High Schools

Distribution of Schools' Average Adjusted 11th-Grade ACT Scores

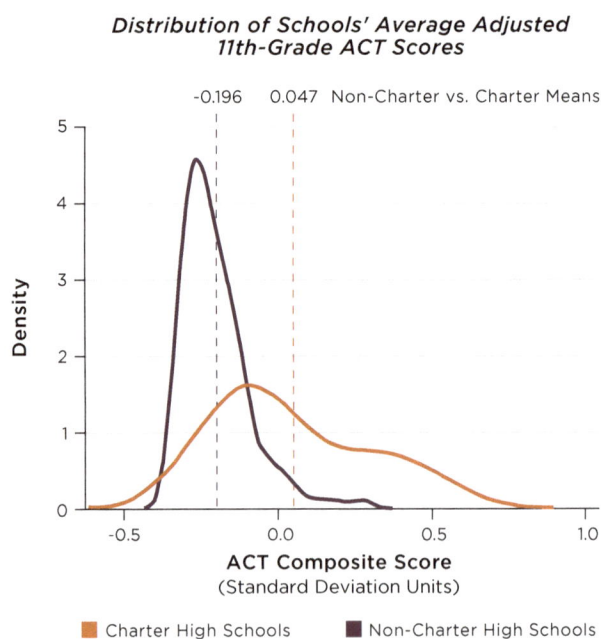

Note: Density plots show school-level residuals from the same 2-level HLM model used to examine overall differences in test scores between charter school and non-charter school students (see Figure 21). These analyses were based on students who were first-time ninth-graders in 2010–13 and controlled for an array of eighth-grade academic performance indicators, eighth-grade school experiences, and background characteristics. Control variables were grand-mean centered so that each school's residual value was the average score for students with typical eighth-grade academic performance, school experiences, and back-ground characteristics.

FIGURE 28

FIGURE 29

CPS Charter High Schools Had More Variation in Average, Adjusted Four-Year College Enrollment Rates than Non-Charter High Schools

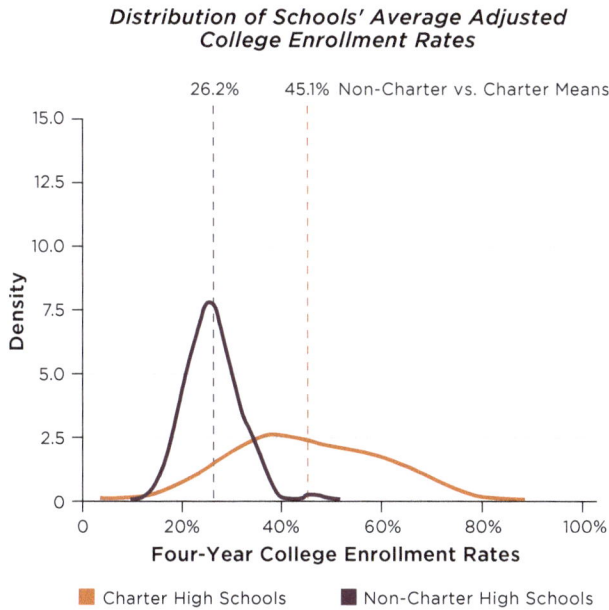

CPS Charter High Schools Had More Variation in Average, Adjusted Rates of Enrollment in Very Selective Colleges than Non-Charter High Schools

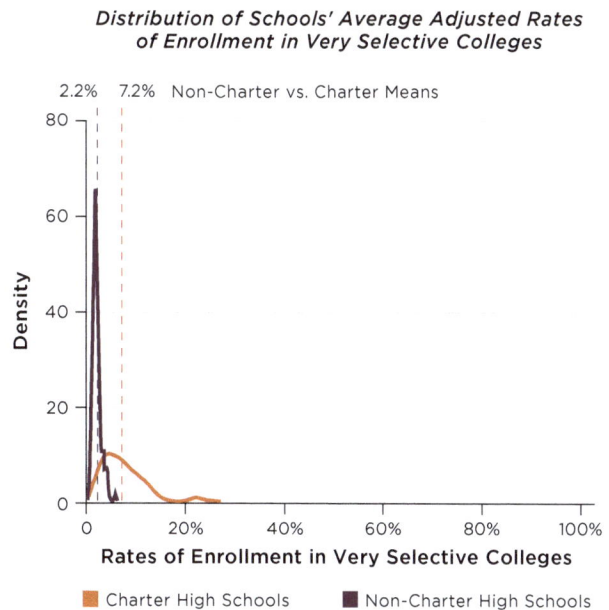

Distribution of Schools' Average Adjusted College Enrollment Rates

Distribution of Schools' Average Adjusted Rates of Enrollment in Very Selective Colleges

Note: Density plots show school-level residuals from the same 2-level HLM model used to examine overall differences in college enrollment rates between charter school and non-charter school students (see Figure 23). These analyses were based on students who were first-time ninth-graders in 2008-10 and controlled for an array of eighth-grade academic performance indicators, eighth-grade school experiences, and background characteristics. Control variables were grand-mean centered so that each school's residual value is the average score for students with typical eighth-grade academic performance, school experiences, and background characteristics.

Note: Density plots show school-level residuals from the same 2-level HLM model used to examine overall differences in enrollment rates in very selective colleges between charter school and non-charter school students (see Figure 23). These analyses were based on students who were first-time ninth-graders in 2008-10 and controlled for an array of eighth-grade academic performance indicators, eighth-grade school experiences, and background characteristics. Control variables were grand-mean centered so that each school's residual value was the average score for students with typical eighth-grade academic performance, school experiences, and background characteristics.

Summary

On average, charter high school students performed better on some, but not all, high school outcomes when compared to similar students in non-charter schools. For example, charter school students had substantially higher test scores and higher attendance. They also had higher levels of classroom engagement, but comparable study habits and grit. Charter school students were less likely to be promoted to tenth grade by their second year in high school, but they graduated from high school at comparable rates to similar students in non-charter schools.

In terms of post-secondary attainment, charter school students generally outperformed students who entered high school with the same academic skills, behaviors, and background characteristics. They had much higher rates of enrollment in four-year colleges and universities and they were more likely to enroll in very selective institutions. Among all high school graduates, charter school students were more likely to

be continuously enrolled for four semesters of college than students who entered high school with the same characteristics. Among only college enrollees, charter school students were just as likely to be continuously enrolled for four semesters as non-charter students.

Some of the practices and policies of charter schools described in Chapter 2 may shed light on overall differences in student performance between charter and non-charter school students. For example, a number of charter schools had more requirements for grade-level promotion, which may be related to their lower promotion rates. Charter schools generally had more requirements for high school graduation, yet their students graduated at comparable rates to students with similar skills and backgrounds in eighth grade. Charter students described their classes as being more academically demanding, which could be related to their higher test score gains, although there were likely to be other factors associated with this as well. Lastly, charter school students and teachers each described their schools as being very focused on preparing students for life after high school graduation, particularly around college enrollment. We discuss the implications of these and other findings in the next chapter.

Findings in this chapter also highlight that not all charter schools were the same. There was considerable variation among charter high schools in terms of test-score performance, college enrollment, and enrollment in selective colleges. Additionally, average performance at many charter schools was much higher than at the highest-performing non-charter schools serving similar students. For example, after taking into account the skills, school experiences, and background characteristics with which students entered high school, average test scores at some charter schools exceeded 0.40 standard deviations, whereas average test scores at the highest performing non-charter school were around 0.30 standard deviations. Similarly, college enrollment rates for typical CPS students exceeded 60 percent in a small number of charter high schools, whereas college enrollment rates in the highest-performing non-charter schools were around 50 percent. Although enrollment rates in very selective colleges were low overall, there were a small number of charter schools that had enrollment rates that exceeded 10 percent; again, higher than the highest-performing non-charter schools serving similar students. There were also some charter schools with very low levels of performance, particularly in terms of average test scores and college enrollments.

CHAPTER 6

Interpretive Summary

The rapid growth of charter schools in CPS has changed the landscape of public education in Chicago. By 2016, 22 percent of students in grades 9–12 were enrolled in charter schools, compared to 4 percent in 2006. As charter schools have become increasingly prominent in CPS, tensions around their existence have grown.

The subject of charter schools often provokes strong reactions from different stakeholders in Chicago. Advocates highlight the possibility of innovation in these schools and tout the strong academic performance of students at particular charter high schools. Opponents voice concerns that charter schools attract the most talented students away from other schools while also encouraging low-performers to transfer out and enroll elsewhere. This study examined each of these issues—charter school enrollments, student performance, school transfers, and organizational features—to determine how charter schools in Chicago were performing. Below we discuss key findings from this study and also highlight the implications that these findings have for all schools in Chicago.

Who enrolled in charter high schools?

The perception that charter schools enroll academically more qualified students is partially right, but not in the way that many believe. Contrary to public opinion, charter schools did not enroll mostly students with high test scores. In a district where there are a number of high school options for high-achieving students, these students were not likely to enroll in a charter high school. But, charter high schools did enroll students with better academic behaviors—including higher rates of eighth-grade attendance and in some cases, higher eighth-grade GPAs—than students who came from the

same neighborhoods and elementary schools. These differences mean that charter high schools started with a population of students that was more likely to attend school regularly than the population at non-charter schools, which is important for promoting a strong school climate.

What does charter growth mean for non-charter schools in CPS?

Additional research is needed to understand how opening new charter schools impacts existing schools in those communities. Nevertheless, given that Chicago's high school population has remained fairly constant over the last 10 years (**see Figure 2 on p.13**), continued charter growth means that non-charter schools have fewer opportunities to enroll students with strong academic behaviors like attendance and, in some instances, grades. This raises the issue of what supports these schools need to remain viable and healthy. Many non-charter schools, particularly neighborhood schools, play a critical role, often serving as centers for their community and providing an education to a wide range of students, including students who may not have strong family supports to explore an array of high school options, students who do not have the academic qualifications to enroll in more selective schools, and students who simply want to remain in their neighborhoods for high school. In recent years, several initiatives have been launched to provide targeted support to non-charter public schools, particularly neighborhood schools.[74] But ongoing support is essential to ensure that they remain strong educational institutions going forward.

How did charter school students compare to similar students in non-charter high schools on a range of high school and post-secondary outcomes?

Students at charter high schools had higher rates of attendance and higher rates of classroom engagement than students in non-charter high schools, controlling for differences in incoming skills and background characteristics. They also had substantially higher test scores. On other outcomes, charter school students performed at comparable levels, or slightly below, similar students in non-charter schools. For example, charter school students had comparable study habits and levels of grit. They were promoted to tenth grade at slightly lower rates than similar students in non-charter schools, most likely because many charter schools had more requirements for promotion.

In terms of educational attainment, charter school students graduated from high school at the same rate as students who attended non-charter high schools, after controlling for differences in incoming skills and background characteristics. This was the case despite charter high schools typically having more graduation requirements than non-charter high schools. Post-secondary outcomes of charter school students, however, were substantially higher than similar students who attended non-charter schools. Among high school graduates, charter students were much more likely to enroll in a four-year college or university after high school, and they were more likely to enroll in very selective colleges and universities, compared to similar students in non-charter schools. Among high school graduates, charter school students were also more likely to persist in college for four continuous semesters. Among college enrollees, however, their persistence rates were the same as non-charter students who entered high school with similar characteristics.

How much variation was there among charter high schools?

Our findings also highlight that not all charter schools are the same. There was considerable variation among these schools on key student outcomes, including test scores, college enrollment, and college selectivity. In fact, there was far more variation among charter schools on these outcomes than among non-charter schools serving similar students. Additionally, the performance of some charter schools exceeded even the highest-performing non-charter schools serving similar students.

Survey results indicated that charter high schools placed a high priority on preparing students academically so that they were ready for college. On average, charter school students described their classes as more demanding than similar students in non-charter high schools, which may have contributed to higher test scores for these students. Charter school students also described their schools as being more likely to engage all students in preparing for their futures. Similarly, charter school teachers described their schools as being more focused on college preparation and on making sure all students were college-ready. Research aimed at understanding the practices and supports used by highly-effective charter schools to prepare their students for college could be useful for many practitioners at all high schools, regardless of sector.

There were also a small number of charter schools with very low average test scores, and low rates of college enrollment. These schools are likely to need intensive support going forward, in order to improve their educational programs and student performance.

Were charter high school students more likely to change schools than non-charter school students?

Despite a number of benefits of attending a charter school, many students who enrolled in these schools in ninth grade transferred out at some point during high school. By the beginning of their fourth year in high school, more than one-quarter of all charter school

---

74 Organizations such as the Network for College Success (NCS) and Generation All both work with neighborhood high schools to support their growth and development. For more information, see https://ncs.uchicago.edu/ and http://www.generationallchicago.org/

students in our study had transferred to another school within the district, most often a neighborhood high school. Even after taking into account differences in incoming skills, school experiences, and background characteristics, charter school students still had higher transfer rates. Transfer rates were highest among charter school students who enrolled in low-performing or new schools, suggesting that these students may have been in search of better educational opportunities. Nevertheless, even in high-performing schools, charter school students were more likely to change schools than non-charter school students. Identifying the reasons why charter students change schools should be a high priority, given that transferring to a new school in the middle of high school can create disruptions in students' educational experiences and potentially place them at a disadvantage as they prepare for postsecondary opportunities. Moreover, since most charter school students transferred into neighborhood schools, this can create a burden for these schools, particularly as they work to ensure that transfer students have the credits they need to be on the path toward high school graduation and college enrollment.

Charter schools were developed with the idea that they could serve as laboratories of innovation that would benefit all public schools. To date, there has been some collaboration between charter and non-charter schools in Chicago,[75] but finding more ways to promote regular citywide conversations between charter and non-charter schools could be beneficial, given the range of performance that exists within both sectors. Many non-charter schools in Chicago have spent years focused on improving student course performance in an effort to increase Freshman OnTrack rates and high school graduation rates. Some of these schools may have insights to share about how to promote strong academic behaviors and mindsets, such as grit and study habits, which could prove helpful to charter schools if they choose to invest more time in developing students' skills in these areas. Similarly, a number of charter high schools have developed strong records promoting test-score growth and sending their students to college. Sharing best practices among charter and non-charter schools could be one way to ensure that there are strong school options for students in both sectors.

---

75 Masterson (2017, July 11).

References

Abdulkadiroğlu, A., Angrist, J.D., Dynarski, S.M., Kane, T.J., & Pathak, P.A. (2011)
Accountability and flexibility in public schools: Evidence from Boston's charters and pilots. *The Quarterly Journal of Economics, 126*(2), 699-748.

Allensworth, E., & Easton, J.Q. (2005)
The on-track indicator as a predictor of high school graduation. Chicago, IL: University of Chicago Consortium on Chicago School Research.

Allensworth, E., & Easton, J.Q. (2007)
What matters for staying on-track and graduating in Chicago Public Schools. Chicago, IL: University of Chicago Consortium on Chicago School Research.

Allensworth, E.M., Healey, K., Gwynne, J.A., & Crespin, R. (2016)
High school graduation rates through two decades of district change: The influence of policies, data records, and demographic shifts. Chicago, IL: University of Chicago Consortium on School Research.

Allensworth, E., Ponisciak, S., & Mazzeo, C. (2009)
The schools teachers leave: Teacher mobility in Chicago Public Schools. Chicago, IL: Consortium on Chicago School Research.

Almond, M. (2012)
The black charter school effect: Black students in American charter schools. *The Journal of Negro Education, 81*(4), 354-365.

Angrist, J.D., Cohodes, S.R., Dynarski, S.M., Pathak, P.A., & Walters, C.D. (2013)
Charter schools and the road to college readiness: The effects on college preparation, attendance and choice. Boston, MA: Boston Foundation and New Schools Venture Fund.

Angrist, J.D., Pathak, P.A., & Walters, C.R. (2013)
Explaining charter school effectiveness. *American Economic Journal: Applied Economics, 5*(4), 1-27.

Balfanz, R., Herzog, L., & MacIver, D.J. (2007)
Preventing student disengagement and keeping students on the graduation path in urban middle-grades schools: Early identification and effective interventions. *Educational Psychologist, 42*(4), 223-235.

Bentle, K., & Marx, R. (n.d.)
Discipline at charter schools. *Chicago Tribune.* Retrieved from http://graphics.chicagotribune.com/news/local/noble-charter-discipline/

Bifulco, R., & Ladd, H.F. (2006)
The impact of charter schools on student achievement: Evidence from North Carolina. *Journal of Education Finance and Policy, 1*(1), 50-90.

Booker, K., Gill, B., Sass, T., & Zimmer, R. (2014)
Charter high schools' effects on long-term attainment and earnings. Working paper. Washington, DC: Mathematica Policy Research.

Booker, K., Sass, T., Gill, B., & Zimmer, R. (2008)
Going beyond test scores: Evaluating charter school impact on educational attainment in Chicago and Florida. Princeton NJ: Mathematica Policy Research.

Booker, K., Sass, T., Gill, B., & Zimmer, R. (2011)
The effects of charter high schools on educational attainment. *Journal of Labor Economics, 29*(2), 377-415.

Bowen, W.G., Chingos, M.M., & McPherson, M.S. (2009)
Crossing the finish line: Completing college at America's public universities. Princeton, NJ: Princeton University Press.

Bowers, A.J. (2010)
Analyzing the longitudinal K–12 grading histories of entire cohorts of students: Grades, data driven decision making, dropping out and hierarchical cluster analysis. *Practical Assessment Research and Evaluation, 15*(7), 1-18.

Brown, E. (2013, January 5)
D.C. charter schools expel students at far higher rates than traditional public schools. *The Washington Post.* Retrieved from http://www.washingtonpost.com/local/education/dc-charter-schoolsexpel-students-at-far-higher-rates-than-traditionalpublic-schools/2013/01/05/e155e4bc-44a9-11e2-8061-253bccfc7532_story.html

Budde, R. (1974)
Education by charter. Paper presented to The Society for General Systems Research.

Bryk, A.S., Sebring, P.B., Allensworth, E., Luppescu, S., & Easton, J.Q. (2010)
Organizing schools for improvement: Lessons from Chicago. Chicago, IL: University of Chicago Press.

Camara, W.J., & Echternacht, G. (2000)
The SAT I and high school grades: Utility in predicting success in college. Research Notes RN-10. New York, NY: College Entrance Examination Board.

Center for Research on Education Outcomes (CREDO). (2009)
Multiple choice: Charter school performance in 16 states. Stanford, CA: CREDO.

Center for Research on Education Outcomes (CREDO). (2013)
National charter school study. Stanford, CA: CREDO.

Center for Research on Education Outcomes (CREDO). (2015)
Urban charter school study report on 41 regions. Stanford, CA: CREDO.

Chicago Tribune. (2014, February 27)
Do charters expel too many students? *Chicago Tribune.* Retrieved from http://articles.chicagotribune.com/2014-02-27/opinion/ct-charter-expulsion-bombshell-edit-0227-jm-20140227_1_charters-neighborhood-schools-expulsion

Cochran, W.G., & Rubin, D.B. (1973)
Controlling bias in observational studies: A review. *Sankhyā: The Indian Journal of Statistics, Series A, 35*(4), 417-446.

Deming, D. (2014)
Using school choice lotteries to test measures of school effectiveness. *American Economic Review: Papers & Proceedings 104*(5), 406-411.

Dobbie, W., & Fryer, R.G., Jr. (2013)
Getting beneath the veil of effective schools: evidence from New York City. *American Economic Journal: Applied Economics 5*(4), 28-60.

Editorial Projects in Education Research Center. (2016, March 31)
Issues A-Z: The Every Student Succeeds Act: An ESSA overview. *Education Week.* Retrieved from http://www.edweek.org/ew/issues/every-student-succeeds-act/

Farrington, C.A., Roderick, M., Allensworth, E., Nagaoka, J., Keyes, T.S., Johnson, D.W., & Beechum, N.O. (2012)
Teaching adolescents to become learners: The role of noncognitive factors in shaping school performance. Chicago, IL: University of Chicago Consortium on Chicago School Research.

Fitzpatrick, L. (2016, October 17)
Chicago could become first city to bargain cap on charter schools. *Chicago Sun-Times.* Retrieved from https://chicago.suntimes.com/politics/chicago-could-become-first-city-to-bargain-cap-on-charter-schools/

Fitzpatrick, L. (2017, March 3)
Noble charter school staff seek to unionize. *Chicago Sun Times.* Retrieved from http://chicago.suntimes.com/news/noble-charter-school-staff-seek-to-unionize/

Friedman, B. (2016, March 2)
State commission overturns CPS decision to close 3 low-performing charters. *Chicago Tonight.* Retrieved from http://chicagotonight.wttw.com/2016/03/02/state-commission-overturns-cps-decision-close-3-low-performing-charters

Fryer, R.G., & Dobbie, W. (2015)
The medium-term impacts of high-achieving charter schools. *Journal of Political Economy, 123*(5), 985-1037.

Garcia, D.R., McIlroy, L., & Barber, R.T. (2008)
Starting behind: A comparative analysis of the academic standing of students entering charter schools. *Social Science Quarterly, 89*(1), 199-216.

Gasper, J., DeLuca, S., & Estacion, A. (2012)
Switching schools: Reconsidering the relationship between school mobility and high school dropout. *American Educational Research Journal, 49*(3), 487-519.

Geiser, S., & Santelices, M.V. (2007)
Validity of high-school grades in predicting student success beyond the freshman year (Research and Occasional Paper Series No. CSHE.6.07). Berkeley, CA: University of California, Berkeley, Center for Studies in Higher Education.

Hamilton, L., & Guin, K. (2006)
Understanding how families choose schools. In J.R. Betts & T. Loveless (Eds). *Getting choice right: Ensuring equity and efficiency in education policy* (pp. 40-60). Washington, DC: The Brookings Institute.

Hanushek, E.A., Kain, J.F., Rivkin, S.G., & Branch, G.F. (2007)
Charter school quality and parental decision making with school choice. *Journal of Public Economics, 91(5-6),* 823-848.

Harris, D., & Larsen, M. (2016)
The effects of the New Orleans post-Katrina school reforms on student academic outcomes. New Orleans, LA: Education Research Alliance for New Orleans.

Henig, J.R. (1995)
Race and choice in Montgomery County, Maryland, magnet schools. *Teachers College Record, 96*(4), 729-734.

Hoffman, J.L., & Lowitzki, K.E. (2005)
Predicting college success with high school grades and test scores: Limitations for minority students. *Review of Higher Education, 28*(4), 55-474

Hoxby, C.M. (2003)
School choice and school productivity (or could school choice be the tide that lifts all boats?). In C.M. Hoxby (Ed.), *The economics of school choice* (pp. 11-67). Chicago, IL: University of Chicago Press.

Hoxby, C.M., Murarka, S., & Kang, J. (2009)
How New York City's charter schools affect achievement, August 2009 report. Cambridge, MA: New York City Charter Schools Evaluation Project.

Hoxby, C.M., & Rockoff, J.E. (2004)
The impact of charter schools on student achievement. Unpublished paper. Cambridge, MA: Department of Economics, Harvard University.

Illinois State Charter School Commission. (2015)
Frequently asked questions. Retrieved from http://206.166.105.35/SCSC/pdf/faq.pdf

Joravsky, B. (2013, December 31)
Rahm creates a process to endorse his plan for more charter schools. *Chicago Reader.* Retrieved from http://www.chicagoreader.com/chicago/advisory-group-endorses-mayors-charter-school-plan/Content?oid=12001029

Kleitz, B., Weiher, G.R., Tedin, K., & Matland, R. (2000)
Choice, charter schools, and household preferences. *Social Science Quarterly, 81*(3), 846-849.

Klugman, J., Gordon, M.F., Sebring, P.B., & Sporte, S.E. (2015)
A first look at the 5Essentials in Illinois schools. Chicago, IL: University of Chicago Consortium on Chicago School Research.

Lee, V.E., Croninger, R.G., & Smith, J.B. (1996)
Equity and choice in Detroit. In B. Fuller & R.F. Elmore (Eds.), *Who chooses, who loses? Culture, institutions, and the unequal effects of school choice* (pp. 70-94). New York, NY: Teachers' College Press.

Leithwood, K., Louis, K.S., Anderson, S., & Wahlstrom, K. (2004)
How leadership influences student learning. New York, NY: Center for Applied Research and Educational Improvement, Ontario Institute for Studies in Education, and the Wallace Foundation.

Louis, K.S., Marks, H., & Kruse, S. (1996)
Teachers' professional community in restructuring schools. *American Educational Research Journal, 33*(4), 757-98.

Lubienski, C. (2003)
Innovation in education markets: Theory and evidence on the impact of competition and choice in charter schools. *American Educational Research Journal, 40*(2), 395-443.

Masterson, M. (2017, July 11)
A common language: Chicago charter sharing its bilingual program. *Chicago Tonight.* Retrieved from http://chicago-tonight.wttw.com/2017/07/11/common-language-chicago-charter-sharing-its-bilingual-program

McLaughlin, M., & Talbert, J. (2006)
Building school-based teacher learning communities: Professional strategies to improve student achievement. New York, NY: Teachers College Press.

Nagaoka, J., & Healey, K. (2016)
The educational attainment of Chicago Public Schools students: 2015: A focus on four-year college degrees. Chicago, IL: University of Chicago Consortium on School Research

Nichols-Barrer, I., Gill, B.P., Gleason, P., & Tuttle, C. (2012)
Student selection, attrition, and replacement in KIPP middle school. Washington, DC: Mathematics Policy Institute.

Perez Jr., J. (2016, March 1)
State commission overrules Chicago Public Schools on 3 charters. *Chicago Tribune.* Retrieved from http://www.chicagotribune.com/news/ct-chicago-school-charter-appeal-met-20160301-story.html

Perez Jr., J. (2016, March 23)
CPS sues state charter panel over reversal of district bid to shut 3 schools. *Chicago Tribune.* Retrieved from http://www.chicagotribune.com/news/ct-chicago-schools-sues-state-commission-0324-20160323-story.html

Renzulli, L., Parrott, H.M., & Beattie, I.R. (2011)
Racial mismatch and school type: Teacher satisfaction and retention in charter and traditional public schools. *Sociology of Education, 84*(1), 23-48.

Reyes, M.R., Brackett, M.A., Rivers, S.E., White, M., & Salovey, P. (2012)
Classroom emotional climate, student engagement and academic achievement. *Journal of Educational Psychology 104*(3), 700-712.

Ravitch, D. (2016)
The death and life of the great American school system: how testing and choice are undermining education. New York, NY: Basic Books.

Rothstein, R. (2004)
Class and schools: Using social, economic, and educational reform to close the black-white achievement gap. New York, NY: Teachers College Press.

Sanchez, M. (2016, April 22)
Walton Foundation stops funding Chicago charters. *Chicago Reporter.* Retrieved from http://chicagoreporter.com/walton-foundation-stops-funding-chicago-charters/

Schemo, D.J. (2004, August 17)
Charter schools trail in results, U.S. data reveals. *New York Times.* Retrieved from http://www.nytimes.com/2004/08/17/us/charter-schools-trail-in-results-us-data-reveals.html?mcubz=0

Sebastian, J., & Allensworth, E. (2013)
How do secondary principals influence teaching and learning? *Principal's Research Review, 8*(4), 1-5.

Shanker, A. (1988, March 31)
Address to national press club, Presented to the national Press Club Luncheon, Washington, DC.

Shanker, A. (1988, July 10)
A charter for change. *New York Times*, p. E7.

Smrekar, C., & Goldring, E. (1999)
School choice in urban America: Magnet schools and the pursuit of equity. New York, NY: Teachers College Press.

Strauss, V. (2012, 2 February)
Ravitch: Why states should say 'no thanks' to charter schools. *Washington Post.* Retrieved from https://www.washingtonpost.com/blogs/answer-sheet/post/ravitch-why-states-should-say-no-thanks-to-charter-schools/2012/02/12/gIQAdA3b9Q_blog.html

Sutton, A., Muller, C., & Langenkamp, A. (2013)
High school transfer students and the transition to college: timing and the structure of the school year. *Sociology of Education, 86*(1), 63-82.

Teske, P., & Schneider, M. (2001)
What research can tell policymakers about school choice. *Journal of Policy Analysis and Management, 20*(4), 609-31.

Tuttle, C.T., Gill, B., Gleason, P., Knechtel, V., Nichols-Barrer, I., & Resch, A. (2013)
KIPP middle schools: Impacts on achievement and other outcomes. Washington, DC: Mathematica Policy Research.

Winters, M. (2015)
Pushed out? Low-performing students and New York City charter schools. New York, NY: Manhattan Institute.

Zimmer, R., & Buddin, R. (2006)
Charter school performance in urban districts. *Journal of Urban Economics, 60*(2), 307-326.

Zimmer, R.W., & Guarino, C.M. (2013)
Is there empirical evidence that charter schools "push out" low-performing students? *Educational Evaluation and Policy Analysis, 35*(4), 461-480.

Zimmer, R., Gill, B., Booker, K., Lavertu, S., Sass, T., & Witte, J. (2009)
Charter schools in eight states: Effects on achievement, attainment, integration, and competition. Santa Monica, CA: RAND.

Appendix A
Data and Methods

Data and Sample

This report used data on several cohorts of first-time ninth-grade students enrolled in CPS schools, excluding alternative schools or special education schools. Data on the 2013–14 cohort was used in Chapter 3, in the comparison of incoming characteristics of students who enrolled in charter schools and students from the same feeder pool. For the analysis of high-school transfers (Chapter 4) and high-school performance (Chapter 5), we examined data on four cohorts of first-time ninth-graders (2010–11 through 2013–14), who were also enrolled in CPS the year prior—a total number of 103,508 students enrolled in 147 high schools, of which 46 were charters. Multiple cohorts were examined in order to mitigate the influence of any random year-to-year differences on our estimates. For the analysis of educational attainment, including high-school graduation and post-secondary outcomes (Chapter 5), we examined data on three earlier cohorts of first-time ninth-graders (2008–09 through 2010–11, for a total of 81,257 students enrolled in 133 high schools, 36 of which were charters). These earlier cohorts were used for post-secondary outcomes because not enough time had passed to allow for the more recent set of cohorts to enroll and persist in college. **Tables A.1 and A.2** provide descriptive summaries of the 2010–11 through 2013–14 freshman cohort sample and the 2008–09 through 2010–11 freshman cohort sample, respectively.

Constructing a Feeder Pool Comparison Group

The analyses reported in Chapter 3 relied on the construction of a feeder pool for each charter high school in CPS. To create each feeder pool, we ran a series of logistic regressions in which the probability of attending a given charter school was modeled as a function of students' elementary schools and neighborhood census blocks. Each analysis was run using the full sample of 2013 ninth-grade students described above, with the exception of students who enrolled in selective enrollment

high schools that were open in fall of 2013. We removed selective enrollment school students from the sample because they were distinctly different from other students, with substantially higher incoming skills and stronger academic behaviors, and as a result, they could not reasonably be considered potential charter school students. Including them in the feeder pool would have artificially boosted the incoming qualifications of the feeder pool.

To calculate the average score on incoming skills and behaviors for each charter school, we included all students in the district who did not attend that high school, but weighted them using the propensity scores from each logistic regression described above. In other words, only those students who had a probability greater than 0 of attending that school were actually included in the calculation of the average statistic. The incoming skills and behaviors of students who came from elementary schools and neighborhoods that sent a number of students to a given charter high school were weighted.

A School Value-Added Model

Our analytic strategy for estimating differences in outcomes between charter school students and non-charter school students used a school value-added model and accounted for a range of differences between students prior to their entry into high school. Equation (1) presents a 2-level hierarchical value-added model in which outcome Y for student i in school j at time t is a function of prior academic performance, eighth-grade attitudes and experiences in school, and neighborhood characteristics corresponding to the student's residence in eighth grade (A), gender and race/ethnicity (X), indicators of eighth-grade student status and school type (S), an indicator for charter school enrollment in ninth grade (Z), and error partitioned at the school (u) and student (r) levels. School-level differences from the average value-added estimate are represented by u_j and are used to generate distributions of school value-added estimates.

$$Y_{ij,t} = A_{ij,t-1}\theta + X_{ij}\beta + S_{ij,t-1}\gamma + \delta Z_{ij,t} + u_{j,t} + r_{ij,t} \quad (1)$$

Descriptive Characteristics for the 2010–11 through 2013–14 Cohorts of First-Time Ninth-Grade Students Enrolled in CPS High Schools

	9th-Grade Students Enrolled in Non-Charter High Schools		9th-Grade Students Enrolled in Charter High Schools	
	N	Mean (SD)	N	Mean (SD)
Eighth-Grade Demographics				
Male	81,157	0.50	22,351	0.51
Black	80,706	0.40	21,514	0.58
Latino	81,157	0.46	22,351	0.37
White	81,157	0.09	22,351	0.02
Old for Grade	81,157	0.18	22,351	0.18
Special Education Status	81,157	0.15	22,351	0.17
ELL Status	81,157	0.07	22,351	0.06
FRP-Lunch Status	81,157	0.87	22,351	0.92
Neighborhood Crime Rate	80,684	0.14 (0.13)	22,152	0.17 (0.15)
Neighborhood Poverty Rating	81,017	0.22 (0.81)	22,279	0.46 (0.79)
Neighborhood Social Status Rating	81,017	-0.43 (0.88)	22,279	-0.43 (0.82)
Enrolled in Catchment School	81,157	0.62 (0.48)	22,351	0.43 (0.49)
Eighth-Grade Academics				
ISAT Math Score	78,847	0.07 (1.04)	22,036	-0.28 (0.79)
ISAT Reading Score	78,567	0.05 (1.03)	22,039	-0.23 (0.84)
GPA Core	74,461	2.64 (0.83)	16,132	2.53 (0.73)
Attendance Rate	80,742	0.94 (0.07)	21,352	0.95 (0.06)
School-Average ISAT Math Score (8th Grade)	81,013	0.02 (0.50)	22,301	-0.13 (0.38)
School-Average ISAT Reading Score (8th Grade)	81,013	0.02 (0.45)	22,301	-0.10 (0.32)
High School Outcomes				
PLAN Composite (10th Grade)	47,377	0.03 (1.03)	10,306	-0.13 (0.84)
ACT Composite (11th Grade)	45,280	0.01 (1.03)	11,741	-0.05 (0.87)
Attendance Rate (9th Grade)	59,557	0.89 (0.15)	16,651	0.93 (0.11)
Attendance Rate (11th Grade)	55,418	0.86 (0.16)	14,348	0.90 (0.14)
On-time Promotion (10th Grade)	77,991	0.95	21,123	0.92
Intra-District Transfer (10th Grade)	75,205	0.07	20,411	0.14
Intra-District Transfer (11th Grade)	71,097	0.13	19,360	0.24
Intra-District Transfer (12th Grade)	50,708	0.18	13,180	0.28

Prior academic performance includes elementary math and reading test scores,[76] eighth-grade GPA[77] and attendance rates, and school-average math and reading test scores corresponding to the student's eighth-grade school. Neighborhood characteristics include measures of the concentration of poverty and social status and the crime rate of the student's neighborhood. Students' prior school climate and experiences are controlled for in the

form of responses to surveys issued while students were in eighth grade and include measures of school safety, student-teacher trust, classroom engagement, emotional health, study habits, and course rigor, among others. We include indicators for prior student characteristics in the form of free or reduced-priced lunch status, special education status, ELL status, and whether a student had been retained in the past. We also include indicators for

---

[76] Predicted eighth-grade test scores based on all observations of prior test scores.

[77] Core courses only (e.g., math, language arts, physical sciences, and social studies).

Descriptive Characteristics for the 2008–09 through 2010–11 Cohorts of First-Time Ninth-Grade Students Enrolled in CPS High Schools

	9th-Grade Students Enrolled in Non-Charter High Schools		9th-Grade Students Enrolled in Charter High Schools	
	N	Mean (SD)	N	Mean (SD)
Eighth-Grade Demographics				
Male	68,570	0.50	12.687	0.50
Black	67,930	0.46	12.156	0.57
Latino	68,570	0.42	12.687	0.37
White	68,570	0.08	12.687	0.03
Old for Grade	68,570	0.22	12.687	0.21
Special Education Status	68,570	0.15	12.687	0.16
ELL Status	68,570	0.07	12.687	0.05
FRP-Lunch Status	68,570	0.86	12.687	0.89
Neighborhood Crime Rate	65,571	0.15 (0.13)	12.309	0.18 (0.14)
Neighborhood Poverty Rating	65,713	0.19 (0.78)	12.340	0.38 (0.78)
Neighborhood Social Status Rating	65,713	-0.37 (0.84)	12.340	-0.37 (0.80)
Enrolled in Catchment School	68,570	0.62 (0.49)	12.687	0.42 (0.49)
Eighth-Grade Performance				
ISAT Math Score	66,542	0.05 (1.02)	12.499	-0.21 (0.79)
ISAT Reading Score	66,209	0.04 (1.01)	12.493	-0.14 (0.82)
GPA Core	63,376	2.48 (0.85)	9.275	2.44 (0.74)
Attendance Rate	67,856	0.94 (0.07)	11.165	0.95 (0.06)
School-Average ISAT Math Score (8th Grade)	68,423	0.01 (0.51)	12.680	-0.08 (0.40)
School-Average ISAT Reading Score (8th Grade)	68,423	0.01 (0.43)	12.680	-0.06 (0.33)
Educational Attainment				
High School Graduation	57,059	0.75	11.305	0.75
4-Year College Enrollment	42,972	0.39	8.459	0.50
Four Semesters of College among High School Graduates	28,977	0.27	5.017	0.29
Four Semesters of College among College Enrollees	11,133	0.71	2,472	0.58
Enrollment in Very Competitive College	16,591	0.17	4.212	0.17

whether a student was enrolled in a magnet, charter, or non-assigned neighborhood school in eighth grade.

All observations were percentile-ranked based on each of the pre-treatment variables denoted by A in the model, and dummy indicators were defined based on these rankings. This resulted in the discretization of each of the continuous pre-treatment variables into nine indicator variables (stanines),[78] with an additional

tenth indicator variable denoting whether an observation was missing for a given pre-treatment variable. The drawback of this approach is that, after modeling their relationships with a student outcome, we are unable to meaningfully interpret the relationship between a pre-treatment variable and the outcome. However, we are not interested in the relationship of the pre-treatment controls with the outcome; we are only interested in

---

[78] Attendance rates were aggregated into five categories (<83%, else <89%, else <95%, else <98%, and else ≤100%).

the relationship between the treatment indicator and the outcome. There is also some information lost when reducing a continuous variable to a series of categorical variables, though with nine categories the amount of information lost is minimal. The benefits to this approach are that we are not forced to remove any observations with missing data. Additionally, the flexibility of this model allows our interpretations of the impact of treatment to be free from any functional form assumptions to which we would otherwise be subject if the model had included the continuous version of pre-treatment variables. For these analyses, the treatment is defined as enrollment in a charter high school in ninth grade. The validity of our estimates as a true measure of the effect of charter school enrollment depends on the assumption that the covariates included in the model fully account for confounding factors related to school quality. The primary concern in measuring charter school performance is that unobserved differences between charter school and traditional public school attendees bias comparisons between the two sectors. Charter school enrollment requires active engagement—parents and students must opt into the sector by choosing a particular set of schools and completing applications, for example. Perhaps there is some factor related both to enrolling in a charter school and later student outcomes that is otherwise unaccounted for by the observed characteristics already included in the model. We believe this to be unlikely given the rather robust set of observed controls included in the model, at least to the degree that it would substantially alter the estimates.[79]

Even for outcomes that occur after ninth grade, a student remains nested in his or her ninth-grade school and is included in the model as long as the outcome is observed for that student. If, for example, a student enrolls in a charter school in ninth grade and by eleventh grade has transferred to another school—whether charter or not—then the observed ACT score for that student will be attributed to her ninth-grade school. Strictly speaking then, for outcomes occurring after ninth grade, these analyses produce intent-to-treat (ITT)

estimates. Values of ITT estimates will be somewhat less favorable for charter schools compared to values of average-treatment-effect estimates because there is a net outflow of students from the charter sector and because transferring schools is a disruptive process that has been shown to have a negative relationship with academic performance. In other words, as few students enrolled in charter schools after their ninth-grade years, associating the observed—ostensibly lower—outcomes of students who transfer with their post-ninth-grade school would result in more favorable estimates for charter schools. Our analyses do not account for this relationship, and thus, the reported estimates for outcomes that occur beyond ninth grade may understate the true effect of attending a charter high school for multiple school years.

We used the same basic school value-added model for dichotomous outcomes except that we specified a Bernouilli distribution and modeled outcomes using a logistic regression. School level residuals from HLMs were used to create the density plots.

Matching Analysis

We performed an additional analysis on the same set of data in which charter school students are matched with students attending traditional public schools on a variety of pre-treatment characteristics. While this approach does not directly obviate the assumption that students who are similar on observed characteristics are similar on unobserved as well, it has been shown to yield estimates that are very similar to those generated by analyses using lottery enrolment data.[80] Lottery studies can proxy the design of a randomized control trial by comparing the outcomes of students who win admission to those who lose and remain in a traditional public school. By virtue of random assignment, it is likely that students who are assigned to attend charter schools are identical, on average, to students who are assigned to a traditional public school on both observable and unobservable pre-enrollment characteristics. And so, in the absence of a lottery analysis—data for

---

79 Estimates related to college outcomes may contain more bias than those related to high school outcomes, as it is more likely that there are unobserved confounding factors associated with a student's likelihood to enroll and persist in a four-year college.

80 Abdulkadiroğlu et al. (2011); Angrist et al. (2013); Dobbie & Fryer (2013); Deming (2014).

which was unavailable to us—we believe a quasi-experimental matching approach to be a suitable comparison.

The matching method draws heavily from techniques used by CREDO (2009, 2013) and Angrist, Pathak, and Walters (2013), in which charter school students are matched to traditional public school students on a combination of characteristics including demographics, cohort, eligibility in special support programs like special education, and prior school. Estimates are then generated using a regression model that controls for prior student demographic and academic characteristics and compares charter school students to their matched counterparts who are enrolled in traditional public schools.

The analysis was performed on the same set of cohorts as the value-added analysis: first-time ninth-graders between 2010–11 and 2013–14 for high school outcomes and between 2008–09 and 2010–11 for college outcomes. In order to construct a comparison group, we first paired each treatment observation with the set of students enrolled in traditional public high schools from the same cohort and who attended the elementary schools from which at least one student enrolled in the same charter high school as the treatment observation. The control set was further reduced to only those students with the same gender, race/ethnicity, age, free

or reduced-price lunch status, special education status, and ELL status as the treatment observation. We then averaged the elementary test scores[81] and outcomes of the up-to-seven matched observations whose elementary test scores were within 0.10 standard deviations of their corresponding treatment observation. This left us with a single, synthetic control observation for each treatment observation whose cohort, elementary school, gender, race/ethnicity, age, free or reduced-price lunch status, special education status, and ELL status was the same as its corresponding treatment observation and whose eighth-grade test score was very similar. In order to check for balance between the two groups, we tested the similarity of the synthetic control observation to treatment observations on test scores as well as on dimensions not included in the matching process.

Table A.3 shows the standardized difference between treatment observations and control observations with respect to elementary test scores,[82] eighth-grade attendance, and measures of neighborhood crime, concentration of poverty, and social status. Outlined by Rosenbaum and Rubin (1985), the standardized difference is defined as:

$$\frac{\overline{x}_T - \overline{x}_C}{\sqrt{(s_T^2 + s_C^2)/2}} \qquad (2)$$

TABLE A.3

Comparison of Pre-Treatment Characteristics Between Treatment and Control Samples Before and After Matching

Pre-Treatment Control	Before Matching			After Matching		
	N (Treatment)	N (Control)	Standardized Difference	N (Treatment)	N (Control)	Standardized Difference
Composite Test Score	22,119	79,380	-0.362	19,829	19,829	-0.001
Attendance Rate	21,352	80,742	0.072	19,017	19,816	0.087
Neighborhood Crime Rate	22,152	80,684	0.237	19,663	19,822	0.042
Neighborhood Concentration of Poverty	22,279	81,017	0.299	19,775	19,828	0.049
Neighborhood Social Status	22,279	80,107	-0.009	19,775	19,828	0.023

Notes: The before-matching control group is comprised of all students in our sample attending a traditional public school; the after-matching control group is comprised of the synthetic control observations created by matching control observations to treatment observations and then averaging across matched control observations for each treatment observation. The composite test score is an average of a student's reading and math test scores.

---

81 Predicted eighth-grade test scores based on all observations of prior test scores.

82 Predicted eighth-grade test scores based on all observations of prior test scores.

Where $\bar{x}$ is the mean of the treatment group *(T)* and control group *(C)*, and s^2 is the pre-match variance of the treatment group *(T)* and control group *(C)*. Prior to matching, the standardized differences for test scores, crime, and poverty between the two groups were relatively large: on average, charter school students had much lower eighth-grade test scores and lived in neighborhoods with higher crime and higher concentrations of poverty. The matching procedure substantially reduced the differences between the treatment and control groups so that the standardized difference on each dimension was no greater than 0.087, which is well below the suggested-guidance threshold of 0.25.[83] Thus, after matching, the control group was similar to the treated sample with respect to observed pre-treatment characteristics—differing only in whether or not they enrolled in a charter high school. To the extent that unobserved differences between the two groups were balanced as a result of balancing on observed characteristics, the control group serves as a suitable comparison for causal inference.

Equation (3) presents an estimation equation in which outcome *Y* for student *i* in time *t* is modeled as a function of prior academic performance, student characteristics, and neighborhood characteristics corresponding to the student's residence *(A)*, gender and race/ethnicity *(X)*, cohort-by-school fixed effects[84] *(S)*, an indicator for charter school enrollment in ninth grade *(Z)*, and a random error term:

$$Y_{it} = \theta A_{i,t-1} + \beta X_i + \gamma S_t + \delta Z_{it} + \varepsilon_{it} \quad (3)$$

Student prior academic performance includes eighth-grade attendance rates and elementary math and reading test scores.[85] We include indicators for prior student characteristics in the form of free or reduced-priced lunch status, special education status, ELL status, and whether a student had been retained in the past. Neighborhood characteristics include measures of the concentration of poverty, social status of residents, and crime rate in the neighborhood corresponding to the student's residence. As with the value-added analysis, students are associated with their ninth-grade school for all outcomes, even those occurring after ninth grade.

Table A.4 presents the estimates of the effects of enrolling in a charter high school in ninth grade for each student outcome that we examined. In general, the results are similar to those obtained from the value-added model, which are presented in Chapters 4 and 5: students who enrolled in charter high schools had higher test scores, attendance rates, and rates of enrollment in four-year and highly competitive colleges. They also had higher rates of intra-district transfer and lower rates of on-time promotion to tenth grade. One difference is that the estimate for the charter school impact on high school graduation becomes statistically significant with the matching model; though, the magnitude of the estimate from both models is small (-0.01 and 0.030, respectively).

Despite the overall similarity in estimates between the two methods, the magnitude of the estimates for test scores and four-year and highly competitive college enrollment is notably larger with the matching model. One possible explanation for this difference is the likelihood that the counterfactual for each method is dissimilar. While the value-added model directly controls for differences in pre-treatment characteristics among all ninth-graders in the district, the matching model compares charter high school students to traditional public school students with similar likelihoods of enrolling in a charter high school based on their demographic characteristics, eighth-grade test scores,[86] and the elementary school they attended. With the matching method, the pool of students from which comparisons could be made is restricted to those who attended an elementary school from which at least one student enrolled in the same charter as a given treatment observation. Charter school students likely attended an elementary school located in the proximity of their charter school, and the geographic distribution of

---

83 Cochran & Rubin (1973).

84 These are not school fixed effects in the traditional sense, as the ninth-grade school attended by the control sample is obfuscated by the construction of synthetic control observations. Instead, synthetic control observations are associated with the ninth-grade school of their matched treatment observation. Because the matching procedure for each treatment observation was performed within-school, there may exist systematic differences in the similarity of matches between schools. We control for any such differences by including these fixed effects.

85 Predicted eighth-grade test scores based on all observation of prior test scores.

charter schools is not random. Thus, if charter schools are systematically established in neighborhoods with the lowest-performing schools, then estimates of their impact will be larger in comparison to those for which the district, as a whole, serves as the counterfactual.

The Estimated Average Difference Between Students Who Enrolled in a Charter High School in Ninth Grade and Those Who Did Not, Based on a Matched Comparison

	Estimate (Standard Error)	Cohorts
PLAN Composite Score	0.251*** (0.032)	2010-12
ACT Composite Score	0.360*** (0.030)	2010-12
Attendance Rate in 9th Grade	0.060*** (0.003)	2011-13
Attendance Rate in 11th Grade	0.062*** (0.003)	2010-12
On-Time Promotion to 10th Grade	-0.018*** (0.005)	2010-13
Intra-District Transfer by 10th Grade	0.071*** (0.005)	2010-13
Intra-District Transfer by 11th Grade	0.075*** (0.007)	2010-13
Intra-District Transfer by 12th Grade	0.055*** (0.008)	2010-12
High School Graduation (4 Years)	0.030*** (0.009)	2008-10
College Enrollment (4-Year College)	0.199*** (0.018)	2008-10
Enrollment in Highly Competitive College	0.131*** (0.015)	2008-10
Four Semesters of College among College Enrollees (4-Year College)	-0.026 (0.015)	2008-09

Notes: Attendance data in the 2010-11 school year were not widely reported by charter schools, so the 2010 cohort was excluded from the analysis with respect to ninth-grade attendance rates only. Estimates were calculated using a model that controls for a variety of pre-treatment student and school characteristics in which treatment observations are matched with a synthetic control observations. Estimates for PLAN and ACT scores are reported in standard-deviation units; all other outcomes are reported in natural units. Standard errors were clustered by cohort and school. Estimates are statistically significant at the ***1 percent level. College enrollment and persistence outcomes are based on the sample of students who graduated from high school; enrollment in a highly competitive college outcome is based on the sample of students who enrolled in a four-year college.

86 Predicted eighth-grade test scores based on all observation of prior test scores.

Appendix B
Supplemental Tables and Figures

Table B.1 shows the number of students enrolled in charter schools by grade level from 1997 to 2016. **Figure B.1** compares average eighth-grade suspensions for students who enrolled in each charter high school to average suspensions for students in the feeder pool. We found that most charter high schools enrolled students whose suspension rates were similar to their feeder pool. Twelve charter schools had students whose suspension rates were lower, on average, than their feeder pools and five charter schools had students whose suspension rates were higher than their feeder pools. **Figures B.2, B.3, and B.4** compare the special education status, English Language Learner (ELL) status, and free-lunch status of each charter high school's enrollees to their feeder pool. Most ninth-grade cohorts in charter high schools had similar proportions of students with disabilities, ELLs, and students qualifying for free lunch as their feeder popula-

tions. Only two schools had special education populations or ELL populations that were substantially lower (more than 5 percentage points) than their feeder pool, while seven charter high schools had populations that were less likely to qualify for free lunch than their feeder pool.

Table B.2 shows regression coefficients and R-squared statistics from statistical models examining the relationship between charter school characteristics and their enrollment advantages. Charter schools with the highest level of prior academic performance and charter schools with the safest environments enrolled students with significantly higher incoming test scores, GPA, and attendance, relative to their feeder pool, than schools with the lowest level of prior performance and schools with the least safe environments. The enrollment advantage of charter schools that were centrally located in Chicago was no different from charter schools that were not centrally located.

FIGURE B.1

Most CPS Charter High Schools Enrolled Students Whose Incoming Suspension Rates Were Similar to Their Feeder Pools

Average Incoming (Eighth-Grade) Suspensions

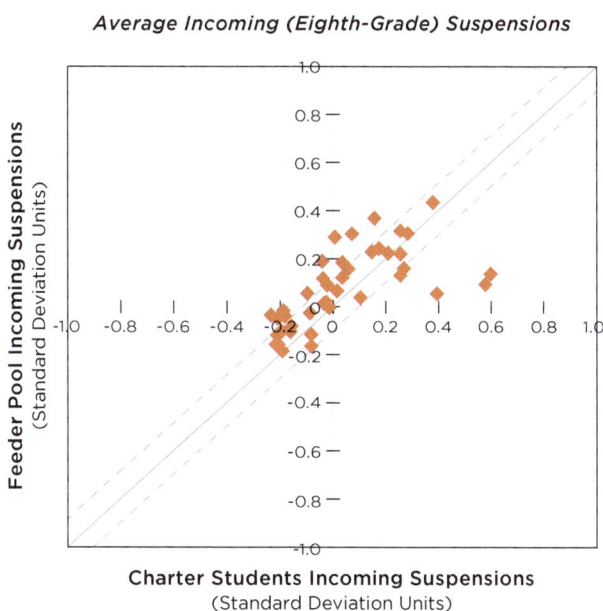

Note: Incoming suspensions of first-time ninth-grade students in 2013-14 were standardized across the cohort. A score of 0 represents the average number of suspensions for this cohort.

FIGURE B.2

Most CPS Charter High Schools Enrolled Students Whose Incoming Special Education Statuses Were Similar to Their Feeder Pools

Percent of Students with Incoming (Eighth-Grade) Special Education Status

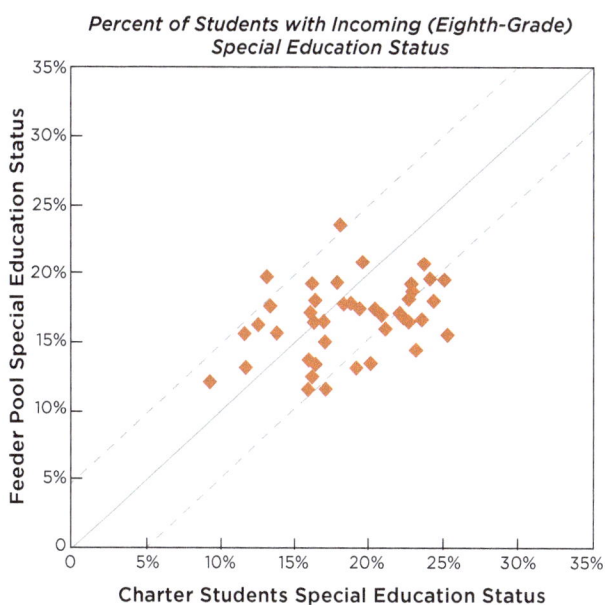

Enrollment Numbers for Charter School Students Enrolled in Charter Schools in CPS, 1996–2006

	Total Enrollment in Grades K-8	Charter Enrollment in Grades K-8	Proportion of K-8 Students in Charter Schools	Total Enrollment in Grades 9-12	Charter Enrollment in Grades 9-12	Proportion of 9-12 Students in Charter Schools	Total Number of Charter Schools in CPS
1996	303,850	0	0.0%	103,172	0	0.0%	0 Elem/0 HS/ 0 Combination
1997	309,106	1,660	0.5%	99,764	319	0.3%	2 Elem/1 HS/ 3 Combination
1998	315,802	2,549	0.8%	96,745	484	0.5%	4 Elem/2 HS/ 4 Combination
1999	320,217	3,386	1.1%	97,143	893	0.9%	6 Elem/3 HS/ 4 Combination
2000	323,274	4,083	1.3%	98,258	1,190	1.2%	8 Elem/3 HS/ 4 Combination
2001	323,069	4,556	1.4%	100,830	1,471	1.5%	11 Elem/3 HS/ 4 Combination
2002	320,708	5,552	1.7%	104,110	1,525	1.5%	13 Elem/3 HS/ 4 Combination
2003	312,139	6,290	2.0%	106,038	2,239	2.1%	14 Elem/4 HS/ 4 Combination
2004	302,744	7,190	2.4%	109,643	2,675	2.4%	16 Elem/5 HS/ 4 Combination
2005	292,492	9,460	3.2%	110,709	3,206	2.9%	23 Elem/6 HS/ 5 Combination
2006	282,864	11,832	4.2%	114,459	4,606	4.0%	29 Elem/10 HS/ 7 Combination
2007	275,942	13,694	5.0%	113,045	6,197	5.5%	31 Elem/16 HS/ 7 Combination
2008	271,222	16,548	6.1%	113,513	9,067	8.0%	38 Elem/20 HS/ 8 Combination
2009	268,956	18,046	6.7%	115,646	11,910	10.3%	39 Elem/23 HS/ 8 Combination
2010	265,408	21,204	8.0%	113,723	15,042	13.2%	43 Elem/28 HS/ 8 Combination
2011	266,036	23,397	8.8%	113,952	17,039	15.0%	47 Elem/27 HS/ 9 Combination
2012	266,527	25,586	9.6%	112,502	19,268	17.1%	49 Elem/29 HS/ 12 Combination
2013	264,845	27,624	10.4%	112,029	20,943	18.7%	53 Elem/32 HS/ 15 Combination
2014	261,801	28,908	11.0%	112,003	21,874	19.5%	56 Elem/32 HS/ 16 Combination
2015	258,697	29,333	11.3%	111,577	23,260	20.8%	56 Elem/32 HS/ 16 Combination
2016	251,654	28,460	11.3%	109,010	23,618	21.7%	52 Elem/34 HS/ 13 Combination

Note: Enrollment numbers only include students enrolled in "regular" CPS schools in each year. They exclude students enrolled in special education schools and alternative schools, including Options schools (e.g., Youth Connections Schools).

FIGURE B.3

Most CPS Charter High Schools Enrolled Students Whose Incoming ELL Statuses Were Similar to Their Feeder Pools

Percent of Students with Incoming (Eighth-Grade) English Language Learner Status

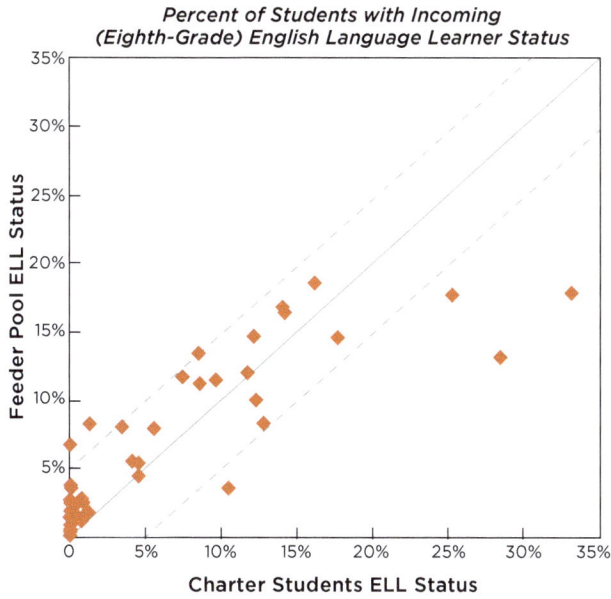

Charter Students ELL Status

FIGURE B.4

Most CPS Charter High Schools Enrolled Students Whose Incoming Free-Lunch Statuses Were Similar to Their Feeder Pools

Percent of Students with Incoming (Eighth-Grade) Free-Lunch Status

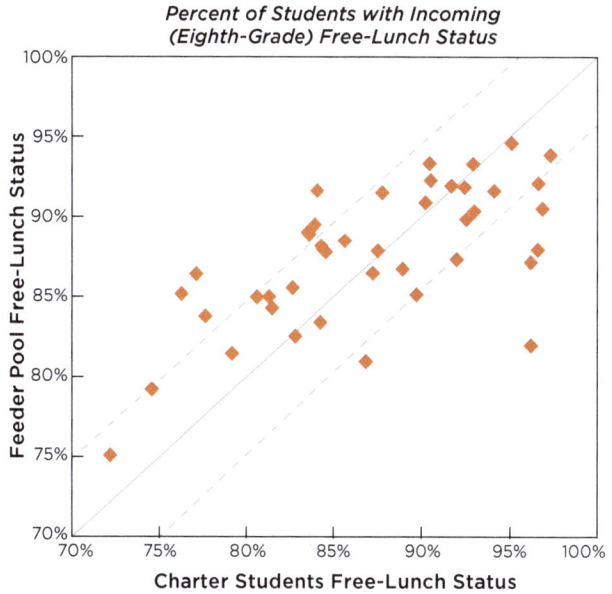

Charter Students Free-Lunch Status

TABLE B.2

CPS Charter High Schools with the Highest Levels of Prior Academic Performance Enrolled Students with Significantly Higher Incoming Test Scores, GPAs, and Attendance Rates Relative to Their Feeder Pools

	Incoming 8th-Grade Test Scores	Incoming 8th-Grade Study Habits	Incoming 8th-Grade GPA	Incoming 8th-Grade Attendance
Intercept (Lowest-Performing Schools)	-0.185	-0.010	-0.132	0.065
Average-Performing Schools	0.122	-0.055	0.036	0.032
Highest-Performing Schools	0.173*	0.033	0.295**	0.023*
No Information Available	0.024	-0.031	0.002	-0.040
R-Squared	0.181	0.096	0.276	0.218
Intercept (Least-Safe High Schools)	-0.162	-0.101	-0.197	0.008
Average-Safety High Schools	0.018	0.040	0.128	0.234*
Safest High Schools	0.119*	0.141***	0.277**	0.182*
No Information Available	0.157	0.100	0.234	0.086
R-Squared	0.152	0.294	0.246	0.154
Intercept (Located Outside of City Center)	-0.104	-0.025	-0.085	0.112
Located Within City Center	0.040	-0.001	0.157	0.060
R-Squared	0.013	0.000	0.091	0.014

Notes: Prior academic performance was measured by first combining two indicators into a single score for each high school in the district: the 2013 high school graduation rate and the spring 2013 ACT scores for students who were in eleventh grade that year. Schools were then ranked and divided into three equal groups: highest-performing schools, average-performing schools, and lowest-performing schools. Schools that were missing this information were grouped into a "no performance information available" group. Only the rankings of charter schools were used for the analysis. The safety level at each school was measured using student responses to an annual *My Voice, My School* survey administered to all CPS students in grades 6–12. Students were asked to describe how safe they felt in the hallways and bathrooms of the school; outside around the school; traveling between home and school; and in their classes. Students' responses were combined into a measure using Rasch analysis, and the measures were aggregated to the school level. High schools were then ranked into three equal groups: Safest high schools, average-safety high schools, and least-safe high schools. Schools that had no safety measure were grouped into a "no safety information available" group. Only the rankings of charter schools were used for the analysis. Finally, schools that were located within three miles of the city center were identified as being centrally located, while all other charter schools were identified as not being centrally located.

Figures B.5, B.6, and B.7 show distributions of schools' average level of study habits, classroom engagement, and grit by sector, controlling for differences in students' incoming skills, school experiences, and background characteristics. Distributions for the two sectors were very similar for each outcome.

Figures B.8 and B.9 show schools' tenth-grade pro- motion rates and high school graduation rates by sector, controlling for differences in students incoming skills, school experiences, and background characteristics. Charter schools had somewhat more variation in their tenth-grade promotion rates, while non-charter high schools had somewhat more variation in high school graduation rates.

FIGURE B.5

CPS Charter and Non-Charter High Schools Had Similar Distributions of Average, Adjusted Student Reports about Study Habits

Distributions of Schools' Average, Adjusted Student Reports About Study Habits

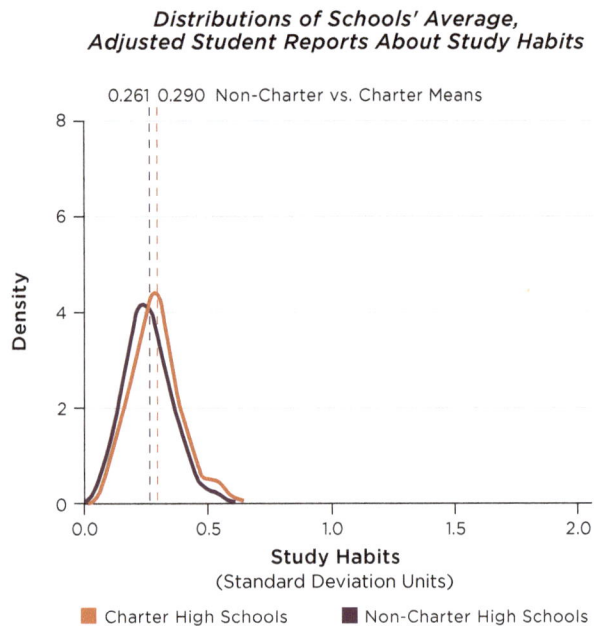

Note: Density plots show school-level residuals from the same 2-level HLM model used to examine overall differences in study habits between charter school and non-charter school students (see Figure 20). These analyses were based on students who were first-time ninth-graders in 2010–13 and controlled for an array of eighth-grade academic performance indicators, eighth-grade school experiences, and background characteristics. Control variables were grand-mean centered so that each school's residual value was the average score for students with typical eighth-grade academic performance, school experiences, and background characteristics.

FIGURE B.6

CPS Charter and Non-Charter High Schools Had Similar Distributions of Average, Adjusted Student Reports about Classroom Engagement

Distributions of Schools' Average, Adjusted Student Reports About Classroom Engagement

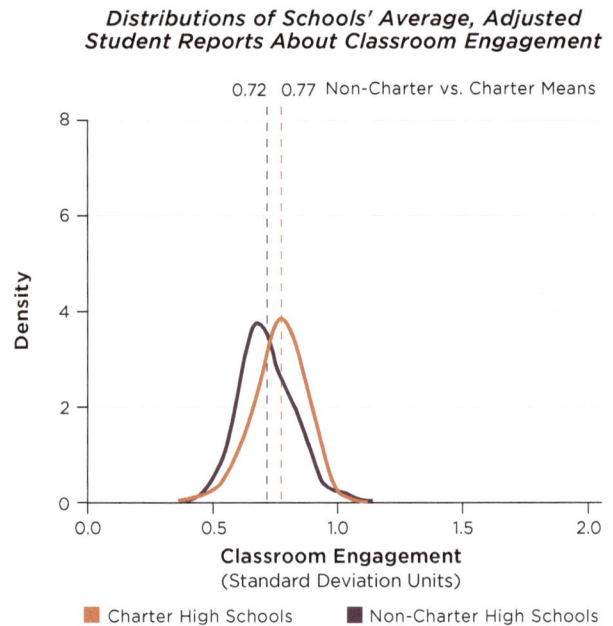

Note: Density plots show school-level residuals from the same 2-level HLM model used to examine overall differences in classroom engagement between charter school and non-charter school students (see Figure 20). These analyses were based on students who were first-time ninth-graders in 2010–13 and controlled for an array of eighth-grade academic performance indicators, eighth-grade school experiences, and background characteristics. Control variables were grand-mean centered so that each school's residual value was the average score for students with typical eighth-grade academic performance, school experiences, and background characteristics.

CPS Charter and Non-Charter High Schools Had Similar Distributions of Average, Adjusted Student Reports about Grit

Distributions of Schools' Average, Adjusted Student Reports About Grit

Non-Charter vs. Charter Means 1.206 1.233

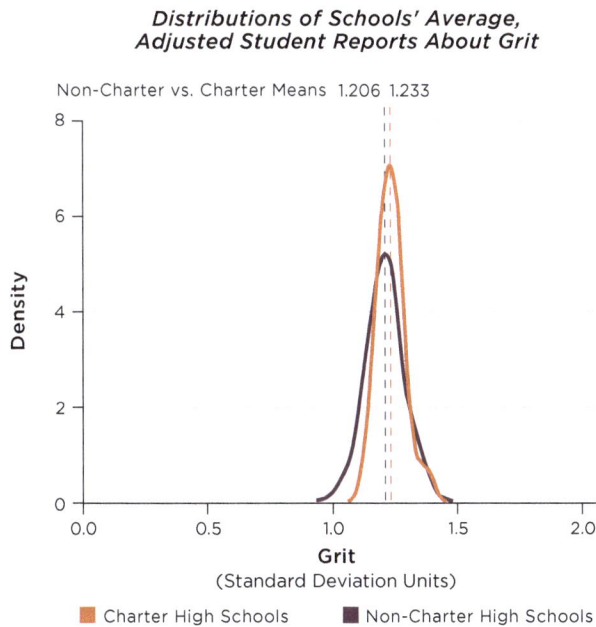

Grit
(Standard Deviation Units)

■ Charter High Schools ■ Non-Charter High Schools

Note: Density plots show school-level residuals from the same 2-level HLM model used to examine overall differences in classroom engagement between charter school and non-charter school students (see Figure 20). These analyses were based on students who were first-time ninth-graders in 2010–13 and controlled for an array of eighth-grade academic performance indicators, eighth-grade school experiences, and background characteristics. Control variables were grand-mean centered so that each school's residual value was the average score for students with typical eighth-grade academic performance, school experiences, and background characteristics.

CPS Charter High Schools Had More Variation in Average, Adjusted Tenth-Grade Promotion Rates than Non-Charter High Schools

Distribution of Schools' Average Adjusted Rates of On-Time Promotion to Tenth Grade

Non-Charter vs. Charter Means 96.1% 98.0%

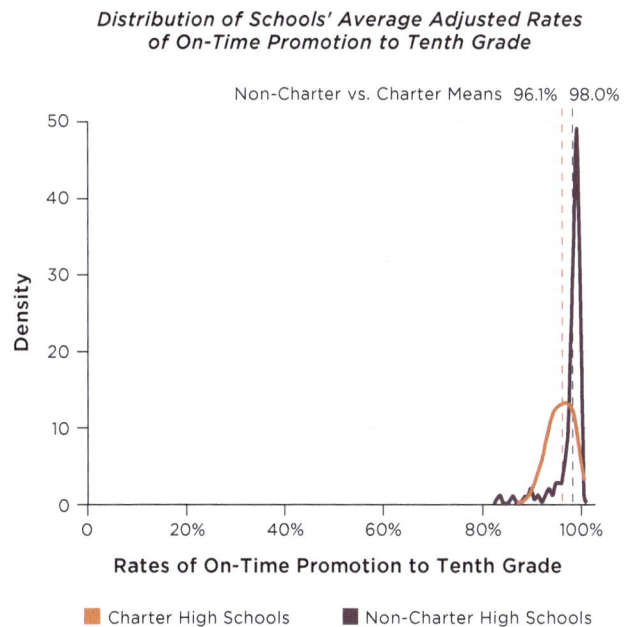

Rates of On-Time Promotion to Tenth Grade

■ Charter High Schools ■ Non-Charter High Schools

Note: Density plots show school-level residuals from the same 2-level HLM model used to examine overall differences in tenth-grade promotion rates between charter school and non-charter school students (see Figure 22). These analyses were based on students who were first-time ninth-graders in 2010–13 and controlled for an array of eighth-grade academic performance indicators, eighth-grade school experiences, and background characteristics. Control variables were grand-mean centered so that each school's residual value was the average score for students with typical eighth-grade academic performance, school experiences, and background characteristics.

CPS Charter High Schools Had More Variation in CPS Charter High Schools Had Somewhat More Variation in Average, Adjusted High School Graduation Rates than Non-Charter High Schools

Distribution of Schools' Average Adjusted High School Graduation Rates

Non-Charter vs. Charter Means   73.0%   73.8%

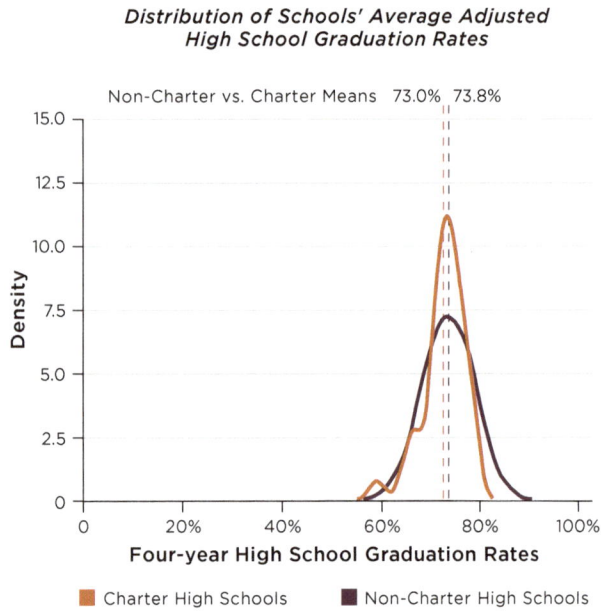

Four-year High School Graduation Rates

■ Charter High Schools   ■ Non-Charter High Schools

Note: Density plots show school-level residuals from the same 2-level HLM model used to examine overall differences in high school graduation rates between charter school and non-charter school students (see Figure 23). These analyses were based on students who were first-time ninth-graders in 2008-10 and controlled for an array of eighth-grade academic performance indicators, eighth-grade school experiences, and background characteristics. Control variables were grand-mean centered so that each school's residual value was the average score for students with typical eighth-grade academic performance, school experiences, and background characteristics.

ABOUT THE AUTHORS

JULIA A. GWYNNE is a Managing Director and Senior Research Scientist at the University of Chicago Consortium on School Research. She has conducted a number of studies examining the skills and academic behaviors students need to be ready for high school and college. She has also conducted research looking at high school graduation rates, school closings, student mobility, and preschool attendance. Her current work is focused on how schools are implementing new science and math standards and whether these standards have an impact on teaching and learning. Gwynne received her PhD in sociology from the University of Chicago.

PAUL T. MOORE was a Research Analyst at the University of Chicago Consortium on School Research at the time this research was conducted. He has substantial experience evaluating the impacts of education policies and is an expert in causal inference with quasi-experimental designs. His research interests include urban school reform, school choice policies and practices, and quasi-experimental design methodologies. Moore has studied historical trends in student performance and school quality in Chicago, has identified indicators of student performance in middle school that best predict success in high school and in college, and has examined the impacts of elementary school closures in Chicago, the impacts of attending a higher-performing high school, and the impacts of attending a charter high school in Chicago. He has co-authored a number of journal articles and reports, and his work is frequently covered in local and national media.